Maurice Taylor

Being a Bishop
in Scotland

the columba press

First published in 2006 by
the columba press
55A Spruce Avenue, Stillorgan Industrial Park,
Blackrock, Co Dublin

Cover by Bill Bolger
Origination by The Columba Press
Printed in Ireland by ColourBooks Ltd, Dublin

ISBN 1 85607 529 X

Acknowledgements

Some excerpts in the section which deals with Central America appeared previously in *New Statesman* and publications of CIIR/SCIAF.

Table of Contents

BEING A BISHOP IN SCOTLAND

Foreword

'When you retire,' people said, 'you'll find that you're busier than ever.' I'm not convinced of that and, perhaps with the idea of giving myself something to do after retirement, I decided to write a book. This is the result.

I hope that, if you read it, you will enjoy it. I have certainly enjoyed writing it. It has allowed me to relive many experiences, to set forth my views on various things, to have my say and tell my story.

My thanks go to those who are part of that story – family, friends, fellow bishops and priests, and many, many others. In particular, for generous help in getting the text ready for the printer, I thank Ellen Hawkes, a good friend, and Harry, my brother.

Maurice Taylor

PART ONE

Being a Bishop in Scotland

CHAPTER ONE

Becoming a Bishop

Since relatively few people become bishops, some details of my experience may be of interest.

On the afternoon of Wednesday 1 April 1981 I was running off some work on the duplicator in Our Lady of Lourdes presbytery, East Kilbride, where I was parish priest. When the phone rang I answered it and was surprised when the voice asked for me and then said, 'The Apostolic Delegate wants to speak to you.' Archbishop Bruno Heim came on and asked me to go to the Delegation in London as he wanted to see me. I said I was fairly busy the following week, would the week after that be suitable? 'No, come this week.' No details of the reason for the summons but I did think it might be either to be bishop of Galloway (I knew Bishop McGee had retired) or to be reprimanded for something wrong I had said or done.

The following morning I told the other priests in the parish that I'd be away all day, drove to Glasgow airport and got a plane to Heathrow. (It was the days of the shuttle service – no booking needed, turn up and go.) At London I was met by a priest and driven to the Apostolic Delegation where I was put into a large empty room. In a few minutes Archbishop Heim came in, eyed me up and down (he did not know me) and then told me that the Holy Father wanted me to be the bishop of Galloway.

Having realised this might well be asked of me, I had decided, if asked, to say 'Yes.' The Delegate told me a story of Cardinal Gasparri (therefore probably early in the twentieth century) having to ask a 'candidate' (the official term) the same question; when the priest said that, before responding, he would like time to consider, pray and listen to the prompting of the Holy Spirit,

Gasparri grew impatient. 'Nothing to do with the Holy Spirit. Yes or no?'

Almost immediately after I said 'Yes', Archbishop Heim, an expert on heraldry, brought up the question of a coat-of-arms and produced a large book to help him give me advice. At that moment I wasn't a bit interested in a coat-of-arms (but I accepted his offer of guidance and it was he who supplied me with the design).

The Delegate invited me to wait for lunch but, as there was still some time before that, I was put in the back garden to walk up and down on my own and think my thoughts.

After lunch (it was roast lamb and I could not help thinking of its sacrificial connotation). I had a further solitary spell in the garden before being taken to the airport. On arrival at East Kilbride, I celebrated the usual Thursday evening Mass which, on that day, was a special one – the silver wedding of two parishioners. I hope I did the occasion justice but my mind was elsewhere and of course 'my lips were sealed'.

At that time I was minutes secretary of the Scottish Bishops' Conference so the following Sunday, 5 April, I had to go to Blairs College for the Lent meeting of the Conference. Archbishop Heim arrived the following day and my appointment was made public at 11am. I do not know whether the bishops already knew of it, or not. But as we were walking along the corridor from the conference room to go to lunch Bishop McGee took me by the elbow and said, 'I'm glad it's you because it might have been someone much worse.' At lunch, my health was drunk and, in my reply, I suggested that my appointment might be seen as a great encouragement for the no longer young since, aged almost 55, I was older than any of the bishops present had been at appointment.

Cardinal Gray and Bishop McGee discussed details of my ordination and decided it would be on Tuesday 9 June (feast of St Columba) at 4pm in the grounds of Fatima House, Coodham (because large crowds would be expected, especially from East Kilbride). Cardinal Gray made a special plea to Archbishop

Heim that he wear his *cappa magna* at my ordination (the last occasion, I think, that the garment, with its hugely long train requiring pages to keep it off the ground, was seen in Scotland).

My episcopal ordination took place as scheduled with Cardinal Gray principal 'consecrator', assisted by Bishops McGee and Thomson; Archbishop Winning preached the homily and my two assistant priests were Mgr Frank Duffy (whom I had asked to continue as vicar general) and Fr John Walls (who had succeeded me as rector of the Royal Scots College in Valladolid). It was a cold day but, although it had been raining earlier, it was dry with some sunshine during the ordination.

I don't remember a great deal about the ordination except for the large crowds, the solemnity of the occasion, the welcome of the people – and the sense of awe which I experienced. I was glad to have been made a bishop but nervous because very aware of my weaknesses and my need for God's grace and the support of my new brothers and sisters of 'Scotland's oldest diocese'.

Very proud to be a successor of the apostles and of St Ninian, I had chosen as my motto the one chosen by another Scottish bishop of two hundred years before, a man whom I greatly admired, John Geddes, rector and second founder of the Royal Scots College in Spain: *'Ambula coram Deo'* means 'Walk in God's presence'. The phrase comes from the Book of Genesis where Abraham is told to leave his country and to walk in God's presence as he goes to the land to which God has chosen to send him.

I like the motto not only for its link with John Geddes but also because it indicates pilgrimage which is the image of the church which appeals most to me.

Needless to say, there have been several attempts at flippant translations. The best, I think, is 'You'll never walk alone'. I have the motto engraved on a ram's horn crozier presented to me. The horn has also a little white house carved into it (*Candida Casa*, another name for Galloway Diocese). I once asked some altar servers if they knew what *Ambula coram Deo* meant. None did, though one imaginative boy had a look at the crozier and its carving and suggested 'Home, sweet home'.

CHAPTER TWO

Renew

After the Second Vatican Council there was a widespread and sincere desire for spiritual and pastoral renewal. We knew that the Council had taught that all of us are called to holiness – but how were we to move towards that? It would be the work of the Holy Spirit, but we would have to co-operate, to be available. But how?

Similarly there was an awareness that dioceses and parishes needed to be communities of faith and committed to building God's kingdom on earth – not just administrative units for governance and convenience or a select group representing and serving the rest.

In the archdiocese of Newark in the United States interesting developments were taking place which resulted in the *Renew* process. *Renew* quickly became popular in many American and Canadian dioceses and not only in Newark. I heard about it while on a visit to the United States and went to Newark to meet the people responsible for teaching the process to those dioceses which were interested in adopting it.

I was very impressed, especially as I was convinced that the vision and hopes of Vatican II for local churches would not be realised without good serious pastoral planning.

Consequently the Newark founder-leaders were invited by me to come to Galloway to explain the process to our priests and parish delegates and then each parish in the diocese was asked whether or not it wished to embark on *Renew*. Five parish priests informed me that their parishes had decided not to take up the offer, but all the others agreed, most of them enthusiastically.

There had been a good atmosphere when the group from

Newark were making their presentations to the Galloway parish representatives. One person told them that she was 'dead chuffed', a phrase that the Americans had to have explained to them.

The upshot was that we sent two people on the next two-months residential course for diocesan *Renew* leaders (Fr Archie Brown and Mr Jim McMillan – the latter by a strange coincidence was born in Newark). They were joined by two people from Glasgow and by other diocesan representatives from Australia and India.

So we embarked on *Renew*. There was a year of preparatory work – explanations to all parishioners, formation of parish teams, training of parish leaders, writing of the material that would be distributed to participants. Then the process proper. Five seasons each lasting six weeks and comprising materials for a) the Sunday Masses, b) small groups, c) large group activities and d) daily scripture readings. Each of the seasons had its own theme: the Lord's Call; Our Response to the Lord's Call; Empowerment by the Spirit; Discipleship; Evangelisation.

Did *Renew* work? How effective was it? Did it make any difference? I would answer these questions positively but with qualifications. *Renew* was more effective when it was carried out well with an enthusiastic priest and widespread involvement (as happened in most parishes). During the five seasons there was a buzz around the diocese because the process engages people and demands time and effort. Moreover, people had to be more involved with each other and to take an interest in scripture, the church's teaching (especially on social issues), the liturgy of the Mass and, of course, the vocation to holiness which we have all been given.

Naturally there were some criticisms. Most commonly, 'too American' because some of *Renew*'s elements were, then, unfamiliar to us, especially small groups but also the ingenious and thorough organisational tools used. New things tend to be resisted and we find reasons for our dislike.

Did *Renew* have a lasting effect? Again, I would say it did.

Initially, I hoped that, once the five seasons were completed, the diocese would continue to offer materials and ideas to the parishes for co-ordinated and ongoing pastoral renewal. But the priests indicated to me that this would be seen as spoon-feeding and would not be well received. Rather, each parish should take responsibility for itself. I am not sure how well such plans were prepared and implemented at parish or deanery level.

But *Renew* gave us some good results that are less obvious: a better appreciation and performance of liturgy, widespread lay involvement in parish activities including the formation of parish pastoral councils, a sense of community in parishes, an awareness of the universal call to holiness, the continuance of small faith-sharing groups.

With regard to the last of these benefits, it was my hope that the small groups might develop into 'small Christian communities'. I had experienced these in Latin America (usually called 'basic ecclesial communities' there) and had heard about similar groups in East Africa. My idea was that they would be truly communities, concerned not so much with political issues (as they were in the oppressive and unjust regimes of Latin America) as with more social concerns, care for those in need, social justice etc, but seen in the light of scripture and its demands. Most of all I hoped that the small groups would not limit themselves to two six-week sessions but would meet throughout the year and that the members of a group would become a true community of mutual concern, friendship and support. The parish then would be a community of communities.

But it didn't happen. Not yet, anyway.

CHAPTER THREE

Yes or No? Decisions, decisions!

On several occasions as bishop of Galloway, I found myself making important pastoral choices that might have seemed unwise at worst, risky at best. Let me list them, reflecting on my motivation and the success (or lack of it) in each case.

Holy Communion under both kinds
Having previously been content with the liturgy of the Mass prior to Vatican II and suspicious of any radical changes, I underwent a 'conversion' in the light of the Council's Constitution on the Liturgy (*Sacrosanctum Concilium*) and its subsequent reception by the church in general and theologians in particular. Above all, I was enthusiastic about the Council's wish that participation should be full, active and understood. This has a number of obvious applications (still not always and fully used) but the one that somehow most caught my attention was the possibility of (frequent) reception of Holy Communion under both kinds by the laity.

There were arguments against (no need, danger of spilling, undue expense) and some people felt intinction (dipping the host in the chalice) was sufficient. But I was convinced that such views were unacceptable. The normal method of human consumption is not by dipping the solid food in the liquid; Jesus told us to eat and to drink (which is a much more complete sign of the sacrament) and, besides, our taking of the Lord's blood expresses our belief that, in holy communion, we are renewing the new and eternal covenant, sealed in Christ's blood.

So, with my encouragement, Holy Communion under both kinds became more and more common in most parishes. We discovered that a) 'danger of spilling' was an unnecessary fear, b) the expense was minimal, and c) the anticipated long queues and undue delays were easily avoided.

The Holy See was granting the required permissions to Bishops' Conferences' requests. In our case in Scotland, the authorisation was generous indeed: 'Sundays and weekdays, as long as there was no danger of irreverence or spillage.' That gave greater impetus to the developing usage and I am glad to say that Holy Communion under both kinds is now practically taken for granted in Galloway, even at our annual pilgrimage Mass at St Ninian's Cave (where the practice is perfectly possible and without any serious danger).

PS: The directive to give Holy Communion to the faithful with hosts consecrated at that Mass (if at all possible) is still, I am sorry to say, not observed as well as it should be. Yet it was Pope Pius XII back in 1950 who urged this practice, and the request has been repeated and explained many times since. The only consolation is that the request seems to be even more widely neglected elsewhere than in Galloway (or Scotland).

Priests' Changes

There is a matter of policy that, like it or not, has very important consequences in practice. It is the question of priests' changes from one parish to another. Canon Law says that priests have a certain right to stability and that they should be asked to move only for serious pastoral reasons. So should the bishop be content to leave priests more or less permanently in one parish or, for the good of the diocese (and of the priests), should there be the custom of priests moving after having been in one parish for a reasonable number of years? Without going into the various meanings that 'the good of the diocese'can have and the variable length of time that would be 'reasonable', my feeling is that, at least in most cases, a priest should be open to transfer, that the reasons in favour of such a policy outweigh the very real arguments that suggest against it. I know also that, when a priest is asked to transfer, it often grieves him greatly, upsets him and the parishioners, and is a serious inconvenience for someone no longer young.

Further, I can truly say that the business of asking priests to move was the most unpleasant task I had as bishop. The ensuing pain for which one is (reluctantly) responsible distressed me. So also the impracticality of consulting parishioners about the qualities their new parish priest should have brought complaints sometimes. The required qualities were always predictable yet, with hardly any priests available, how could the wishes be fully met? And would not consultation be seen then as merely a cosmetic exercise with the decision apparently already made?

Shortly after I came to the diocese and after consulting my predecessor and the vicar general, I made several changes or transfers. They were obediently accepted by the priests involved but there was an impression that I had acted if not unjustly, at least inconsiderately.

One consequence was the appointment of a committee of three priests (whom I asked the Council of Priests to choose) to help me with future changes. I think this worked well enough in general and especially when changes were unavoidable (following deaths etc).

But a very serious situation arose following an assembly of priests of Galloway which we held in 1990. One of its recommendations (not unanimously approved) was that priests should not remain 'for ever' especially in those parishes which were considered among the 'best' in the diocese. When I put this recommendation into effect and asked some priests to transfer to other parishes, they declined. Without going into details, suffice to say that the dispute was finally decided by the church's highest court, the Apostolic *Signatura* in Rome. That court found in the priests' favour, advising me that I had made errors in procedure and that, if I wished to proceed, I should correct such procedural errors. However, since the whole business had already caused bitterness and had been widely reported, I had no stomach for prolonging the dispute.

It was a sad experience for all of us who were concerned and there will always be disagreement about the wisdom, or lack of it, of my actions. Perhaps some day someone will write a thesis on the whole business, examining all the huge amount of relevant correspondence and documentation, and will be rewarded with a canon law doctorate.

But, since 1990 or thereabouts, I confess that I have asked priests to change only when it was necessary and not in cases where I thought such changes would be merely beneficial.

As I said, priests' changes are never easy. For me, they were a source of real distress.

Ministry to Priests

A bishop must have special care of his priests. That has become ever more clearly a most important duty of the bishop. Perhaps like other bishops, I have to confess that I wish I had done more and done it more effectively. May the Lord – and my brother priests – forgive my shortcomings in this respect.

There may have been a time when the personal needs and welfare of priests were not considered or were overlooked or assumed to be each priest's own responsibility.

However, I had not long been in Galloway when I heard of the programme called 'Ministry to Priests", designed in the United States by Fr Vince Dwyer. Although a Cistercian, Fr Dwyer was very aware that diocesan priests needed care, and especially because they did not have the support of a community in the way that priests who belong to a religious order or congregation do.

So, along with Cardinal Winning in the archdiocese of Glasgow, I arranged for the Ministry to Priests programme to be presented to our priests for their consideration. It was a Fr Jim Dyson who came to Galloway and, as a result of his careful explanation, the priests decided to embark on the scheme.

We carried out some written psychological tests (which eventually were returned to us as personal and diocesan profiles), we were instructed in the aims and methods of the programme and told that the programme offered several initiatives (one-to-one ministry, priests' support groups, and a priest chosen by us – overwhelmingly we voted for Canon Nicholas Murphy of St Mary's, Saltcoats – to be co-ordinator of the programme, assisted by others, also chosen by us).

The scheme worked well, especially the support groups which met – and still meet – monthly for an overnight together. Those priests who are in the groups are very aware of the support we receive at our monthly get-togethers.

Eventually it was decided in the 1990s that, since not all the priests had become involved in the Ministry to Priests programme, we should try to widen things so that those priests would not feel that they were in any way excluded from 'ongoing formation' (as urged by the Pope in his 1992 document *Pastores Dabo Vobis*). So, although the elements of the Ministry to Priests programme remain, the priests elected an Ongoing Formation team to arrange retreats, study days etc and to keep an eye on the needs of priests, both individually and as the presbyterate.

I feel that we did as much as we could in this respect and that, if some priests felt overlooked or neglected, the remedy was at hand if they wished to avail themselves of it.

Permanent Deacons

Partly to respond to the decreasing number of priests and partly to restore the practice of the early church, the permanent diaconate was authorised by the Holy See in 1967 and can be introduced by any bishop in his diocese, provided the local Bishops' Conference has agreed.

Permanent deacons are used especially in the English-speaking world, above all in the United States. In Scotland, Aberdeen was the first diocese to train and ordain permanent deacons and, in more recent years, Aberdeen's lead has been followed by all the other dioceses.

Without denying the appropriateness and the usefulness of permanent deacons, I did not adopt this innovation (or, if you like, restoration) during my time as bishop of Galloway. My decision was taken after two consultations with the priests of the diocese (both of which recommended the choice I made).

So, why did I not? Well, principally because I did not want to further 'clericalise'the church. I feel that there used to be too much exclusion of the laity (and especially of women – who, remember, cannot be deacons) from real and active participation in the work and liturgy of the church. It was my suspicion that permanent deacons would tend to increase such lay exclusion.

Secondly, and related to my first reason, I did not see that permanent deacons are empowered to be a real antidote to the shortage of priests. They cannot celebrate the Eucharist, administer the sacraments of reconciliation and anointing of the sick – and much of what they can do can also be done by laity: celebration of the Word with Holy Communion, taking Holy Communion to the house-bound, visiting the sick in hospital and at home, conducting funerals. True, they can read the gospel and preach the homily at Mass – but there will always be a priest there; they can officiate at baptisms and weddings – but these are somewhat infrequent occasions.

Of course, my attitude was not inflexible and unalterable, especially if conditions (or the priests' advice) were to change. Indeed, my successor takes the positive view – which, of course, he has every right to do and which may well be a wiser one than mine.

Christian Initiation of Children

The wonderful and beautiful rite which we nowadays use for Christian Initiation of Adults (RCIA, itself the restoration of a process used in the early church) led to a review of our method of carrying out the Christian initiation of children.

Above all, we re-discovered that the three sacraments which children receive (baptism, confirmation and first communion) are not just three distinct events in a child's life but do form a real and necessary process, namely a child's initiation as a full and active member of Christ's church, the people of God.

Hence, there would seem to be a correct sequence for the reception of these sacraments. Clearly baptism must be first, but then, in the previous experience of most of us, it did not seem to matter if we were confirmed before or after first communion; rather, that depended on the bishop's practice and availability regarding his visits to parishes to confirm the children.

It is evident, however (and for theological and liturgical reasons), that confirmation is the completion of baptism and should

precede first communion, which is the culmination of our children's initiation. This reasoning is confirmed by the correct usage
to be followed with RCIA.

Undeniably, this fact poses problems. There are several practical problems; moreover, we lose the pastoral benefit of seeking
a confirmation commitment which young children cannot
make; and we abandon our traditional way for a possibly unwise innovation.

Over several years the Bishops' Conference discussed, ar-
gued, hesitated. Finally I suggested, and the bishops agreed,
that Galloway diocese be allowed to go ahead, by way of experi-
ment and trial, with a new (or, rather, re-discovered) process of
children's initiation into full membership of the church.
Essentially this meant keeping to the order : baptism, confirmation, first communion; and, of course, retaining infant baptism
and delaying the other two sacraments until at least 'the use of
reason'.

In fact we decided in Galloway that, where previously the
normal had been first communion after Easter in primary 3
(therefore age 7 and 8) and confirmation in primary 6 or 7 (age
10 to 12), we would now have both confirmation and first communion in primary 4 (age 8 + to 9+). Moreover we recommended
that, since the children were becoming full members of the
church (including the local church), it was right that the sacraments be conferred at a Sunday Mass, when far more members
of the local church would be present.

A consequence of this was that I no longer was able to confirm personally many of the candidates. I went to as many
Sunday confirmations as I could and, to maintain as far as possible the connection between the bishop and the sacrament of confirmation, I issued each year an official letter delegating the local
parish priest to confirm in my name and asked that the letter be
read out at the start of the ceremony. In addition I suggested, but
without great success, that I be invited to a class or parish Mass
after the children had been initiated in order that I might ac-
knowledge them as newly full members of the church.

Perhaps surprisingly the whole new arrangement was generally accepted by the priests, the teachers, the parents and the parishes. The RE syllabus in the primary school needed some adaptation but this was carried out effectively by Sister Dorothy McCaffrey SND (our RE adviser for primary schools) and well implemented by the teachers. The new arrangement has now been in operation for several years and is working smoothly.

However, one has to ask whether the process has brought benefits and advantages, or not.

First, it is true that my involvement as bishop was reduced as far as confirmation of most children was concerned. I have already mentioned how I hoped to compensate somewhat for this.

Second, would it not be better to have confirmation and first communion separated? Our reason for not doing so is that, once a person has been baptised and confirmed, he or she is ready for holy communion, can be said even to have a right which should not normally be delayed.

Third, are children of 8 or 9 old enough to understand confirmation? I respond that none of us fully understands the sacrament; that, at whatever age we receive it, our understanding should continue to deepen; that young children can have an appreciation of the sacrament in accordance with their age; and that, taken to its logical conclusion, the objection would raise doubts about infant baptism.

Finally, by not having teenage confirmation, are we not forfeiting a wonderful opportunity for them to make a mature commitment to be faithful? I would reply by suggesting that the success rate of such teenage commitment is very debatable and, more importantly, by insisting that all of us (not only teenagers) need to make such commitments and that the right time to make them is not confirmation (because that is not what the sacrament is for) but at the renewal of baptismal promises each year at the Easter Vigil. In fact I dearly wish that the last point were better understood and carried out!

So, to conclude: our re-discovered process of initiation of children as full and active members of the church is theologically, liturgically and historically correct; the method contains all the potential to achieve great benefits for each person, each family, each parish and the diocese. And it is my earnest prayer that the people of the diocese will seize the opportunity offered to them in the Christian initiation of their children.

Embracing the Future

The obvious decline in the number of priests – and what to do about it – had been a long term concern. During my absence from work (because of cancer, July-December 2002), the Council of Priests commissioned and produced a paper called *Embracing the Future*. This listed what, with fewer priests, the laity had a right to expect of their pastors and also what limitations the latter had a right to put on such demands (and, more positively, what provision should be available to them for their own welfare). The document also asked the priests of each deanery to indicate the deployment of priests in the deanery if a) there were one less than at present; b) two fewer; c) only half the present number.

When I returned to health and to work early in 2003, I was grateful for the priests' initiative and approved of it.

Moreover, I felt that we should build upon that foundation in two ways. First, by encouraging a greater number of lay people to become actively involved in pastoral ministries. Parishes were asked to ascertain their own needs of lay ministries, not only liturgical but also in evangelisation, catechesis, justice and peace, those in need, sacramental preparation; then, keeping their specific local needs in mind, to ensure adequate and proper training as required. For this we provided our Pastoral Ministry Course, a two-year part-time non-residential course of teaching, reading, essays and practical work to give to those who want to minister in their parishes or deepen their knowledge and appreciation of scripture, liturgy, church teaching and social care.

The success of these plans concerning extended and trained lay ministry is perhaps for others to judge. Let me say we have tried our best, we have had some success but probably 'there is still room for improvement'.

The second initiative, built on the foundation of *Embracing the Future* (How are we to manage with fewer priests?), was to take up John Paul II's call, in *Tertio Millennio Ineunte*, for spiritual and pastoral renewal in the local church. The Pope speaks of the opportunity we have after the 2000 Jubilee Year and the beginning of a new millennium but he leaves the details of such a plan of renewal to each local church. I feel that, in Galloway for the years ahead, we can use the five areas highlighted by the Pope and the three activities he recommends as the areas in which the diocese can seek pastoral and spiritual renewal for itself, its parishes and its families: holiness, prayer, Sunday Eucharist, sacrament of reconciliation and scripture; and the activities: the development of communion, evangelisation (including ecumenism) and care for those in need.

These five-plus-three headings are sufficiently wide to allow all manner of practical initiatives in the diocese and in the parishes (or deaneries). The Pope's idea is that the parish should be a community of small communities. The work was only in its initial stages when I was made 'bishop emeritus' but I have great hope that it will be continued prayerfully, conscientiously and faithfully.

The three words 'Embracing the Future' were chosen carefully, especially the first. It indicates not a negative attitude ('We had better do something but we are not sure what') but a truly hopeful outlook to circumstances and conditions which will be very different but full of challenge and opportunity.

CHAPTER FOUR

Accountability

In his 'Apostolic Exhortation on the Formation of Priests' (*Pastores Dabo Vobis*, 1992) Pope John Paul II, in the final chapter, speaks of the necessity of ongoing formation for all priests. Apart from theological reasons (St Paul instructs Timothy, 'I remind you to rekindle the gift of God that is within you'), there are also compelling human reasons. Ongoing formation, says the Pope, 'is demanded by the priestly ministry seen in a general way and taken in common with other professions, that is as a service directed to others. There is no profession, job or work that does not require constant updating if it is to remain current and effective.'

On the same subject the *Norms for Priestly Formation* issued by the Scottish Bishops' Conference (2005) point out that a priest's continuing formation is an obligation. 'In the first place he is answerable to God should he neglect the gift he received at ordination. At the same time he also has a responsibility before his bishop and the rest of the presbyterate, as well as to the people to whom he is sent, to make sure he is as well prepared as possible to do what is expected of him.' (*Norms* 11.1)

So the need for, and the obligation of, ongoing formation are clearly stated. The exact manner in which that obligation is to be fulfilled will vary from priest to priest and from diocese to diocese.

It is not for me to guess how well the responsibility is being carried out. Perhaps it is enough to say that for many of us – or most of us – we are aware of the need and the duty, we are doing something to respond, but 'there is still room for improvement'.

A related subject that has often exercised my thoughts is the accountability of priests and bishops – and to whom are we accountable? To God, certainly; we shall all be called to 'give an account of our stewardship'. To whom else? To the church, surely; that is, to those whom the priest or bishop is sent to serve.

Accountability is concerned not only with the duty of seeking ongoing formation or attending in-service courses. It includes these but is wider. It is about competence, commitment, fulfilment of one's responsibilities, doing a good job, giving 'value for money'.

At present this is largely left to a priest's (or bishop's) own conscience. Parishioners may feel dissatisfied, a few may even write to the bishop to complain. But, except in cases of serious dereliction of duty, the bishop (or, indeed, the Holy See) will do little more than exhort and hope that things will improve. Apart from the canonical protection that priests and bishops have against sanctions, priests are very scarce nowadays ...

Sometimes I have felt unhappy about this apparent freedom that we have from any real accountability (in this life). More seems to be demanded in Reformed churches.

In the Church of Scotland, for example, a parish does not have to 'take what it gets' but, at least, ministers have to apply for positions and a parish decides whether it wants the applicant. I am afraid that this would not work in the Catholic Church with our diocesan structures and with priests constrained to working in the diocese for which they have been ordained. The diocese has an obligation to look after all its priests (unless they have chosen to leave the active ministry) and the idea of having to support priests whom no parish community wants is practically unthinkable for the poor (in more senses than one) bishop.

I remember an occasion, before I became a bishop, asking a bishop (now dead) what he did if and when there was an incompetent or lazy priest – did he move him to another parish? 'No', he replied, 'better to have one (possibly) unhappy parish than two.' That, incidentally, is merely by way of being anecdotal.

Many professional people and/or institutions are now subject to published league tables. I don't know if that would work for priests (or bishops) and parishes (or dioceses). At the very least it would be good if there were some recognisable and objective standards against which we could be measured. But are there? And would we consent to be judged? And who would do the judging?

Perhaps there has been too much negativity in what I have said – going after those who seem to be failing. So, to be positive also, I think it would be good for priests and bishops to have 'supervision'in the sense of someone, properly qualified, to listen to a man (in private), to ask wise questions, to explore with him sensitive areas about his work, to advise, to encourage and so on.

This would require qualified people to be available as well as priests and bishops willing to have supervision. We are a long way from that at present, but could we not try to make a start? It would help those who would welcome such an opportunity – and it would assuage the unease, or guilt, of bishops like me!

CHAPTER FIVE

Schools

Children in school are something of a captive audience for the priest (or bishop) who wants to visit. Despite that, it was my pleasure to pay an annual visit to all the primary schools in the diocese (37 of them in 1981 but five or six had been closed by 2004). On each occasion I tried to visit each class in the school, a task which in the bigger schools occupied practically the whole day.

Depending on the age of the children I attempted to say something religious but not to the exclusion of showing an interest in the children's lives or projects and to share nursery rhymes (with infants) or to give friendly 'tests' (to the older children). In the early days I also tried to tell a joke or pose a riddle but I stopped that when the children would ask if I wanted to hear their jokes and one girl regaled us with a joke which embarrassed the class teacher and me, though it was greatly enjoyed by the other children. In the classes in which the children were preparing for First Holy Communion or Confirmation I tried to say something appropriate and, from time to time, I invited the children in the confirmation class to write to me telling me about their preparation and asking me to confer the sacrament on them. Here are some of the letters I received:

'I am now 11. Over the past ten years my faith has been going up and down. If you confirm me, it will go up and stay there. Please confirm me and stop this yo-yo of love and hate.' (John, Kilbirnie)

'I especially want to be confirmed by you because, to me, you're the next best thing to God or the Pope.' (Martin, Troon)

'I am hoping to get better from the confirmation by helping others and not to be so mean and cruel to my little brother. Also around the home I don't usually help but this great occasion will bring me back to my senses, I hope.' (Debbie, Cumnock)

'I wish to be confirmed. I feel I am ready to become a member of the Christian community. I have been going to church now for eleven years. Ten of these years meant nothing to me. I hope my wish is granted.' (Margaret, Irvine)

And a post- Confirmation verdict:

'I enjoyed my confirmation more than I thought I would. I am very glad you have a gentle hand. When we practised for confirmation I found that Father … hasn't got a gentle hand.' (Alice, Kilmarnock)

In general children in primary schools were open, friendly and talkative. On one occasion when I arrived at a school, it was the morning interval and the children were in the playground. As they gathered round, I asked one child 'Who's your teacher?' 'Fine' was the prompt reply.

I am afraid that I was not so conscientious in visiting the Catholic secondary schools (seven in 1981 but only five in 2004 and soon to be four). It wasn't only because in secondary schools the children move constantly from room to room while primary children are more static. I just found that I got very little response from the older children and I suppose I wasn't brave enough to persevere, except if I was asked by the head teacher to visit a fifth or six year class. Such 'by appointment' visits were pleasant for me and, I hope, for the pupils.

There are no Catholic special schools (schools for pupils with special needs) in the Galloway diocese but I did try to visit all the non-denominational special schools every year or two. When I first began this custom, I think some of the head teachers were a little suspicious of my motives but, as I got to know them, I believe I became a welcome visitor. I used to receive invitations to their Christmas plays and carol concerts and, on one occasion, I was invited to have lunch with the older pupils, eating what they themselves had cooked.

Teachers, in fact, I always found unfailingly welcoming and, over the years, I think we got to know one another and in many cases have become friends. I hope I am also friends of the pupils although, since they grow and change rapidly, I confess that, after a while, I find it difficult to recognise them again. May they forgive me for the apparent and unintended discourtesy.

CHAPTER SIX

Bishops' Conference

It seems natural for all the bishops of a country to meet from time to time. Nowadays such meetings, and indeed the institution of bishops' conferences, are enshrined in the law of the church.

'The Bishops' Conference is the assembly of the bishops of a country ... exercising together certain pastoral offices for Christ's faithful of that territory.' (*Code of Canon Law* no 447) 'The Bishops' Conference can make general decrees only in cases where the universal law has so prescribed or by special mandate of the Apostolic See ... (otherwise) the competence of each diocesan bishop remains intact.' (*Code of Canon Law* no 455)

So except on rare occasions a bishops' conference does not make laws; it exists principally for pastoral and administrative purposes.

There are eight dioceses in Scotland and so normally there are eight members of the Bishops' Conference of Scotland (a few more if and when there are also some auxiliary bishops). The Scottish Conference has two three-day statutory meetings (in Lent and in November) and, in addition, five or six overnight meetings. Meetings take place nowadays in Scotus College, the national seminary situated in Bearsden, Glasgow.

Meetings of our Bishops' Conference I normally enjoyed. The principal reason for this was the companionship. We were, indeed are, a band of brothers who get on well together. With only eight members, we know one another well, are on first name terms, are relaxed in each other's company. The meetings have also become more informal than when I first joined the Conference.

There is, moreover, a sense of satisfaction that we can share each other's concerns and try our best to do a useful job. The amount of work to be done keeps increasing, and so, worryingly, do costs. Since these costs are raised by levies on each diocese, we are constantly in a dilemma: we ought, for example, to set up another commission, employ a new professional, take on extra commitments: yet is it right, or even possible, for the dioceses to meet the increased expense? Also, there is the need to avoid unnecessary expense and to be as sure as we can be that we are getting value for money.

Our agenda seemed constantly and ineluctably to get longer and longer. That put us under pressure and it was the president's responsibility, as chairperson, to keep things moving, to try to limit digressions and unnecessary discussion and to ensure that we reached, where required, a clear and agreed decision. Some chairmen were better than others at these tasks so it would be wrong to imply that the Conference never suffered frustration or that there were never moments of irritation and tension.

To give you an idea of the agenda, here are some of the items discussed: our seminaries, the various national commissions and other agencies of the Conference (about twelve or fifteen of them), items received from the Vatican, matters concerning schools, ecumenical relations, various issues of the day (usually of an ethical or moral nature), pastoral planning, the needs of priests, and correspondence (sometimes weird and wonderful).

The Conference has the valuable help of its General Secretary, its Minutes Secretary and its Media Officer and most meetings involve receiving personal reports from various persons or groups (seminary rectors, commission presidents, lawyers etc).

I don't think that either the role or the work of our Scottish Bishops' Conference is well recognised and I sometimes wished that (a) our published bulletins were more widely distributed and read by priests and people and (b) the Conference would speak out more often on national and international issues so that the voice of the Catholic Church in Scotland would be heard more clearly. We could not expect that all our statements would escape criticism but, as has often been said, 'There is no such thing as bad publicity.'

As a postscript to what I have said about the Bishops' Conference, let me mention something called 'The Mount Carmel Group' meetings. These are held twice yearly, each bishop being accompanied by three of his close pastoral advisors (clerical or lay). The Mount Carmel Group's purpose is to share pastoral ideas and initiatives, to plan common pastoral activities, to discuss and decide pastoral priorities. Such topics as *Marriage and the Family*, *Preparing for and Celebrating the Millennium*, *Being the Church in Today's World* have occupied our attention. The agenda is always pastoral and, on the whole, I think most of us consider the meetings to have proved worthwhile.

Why 'Mount Carmel'? Because the first meetings were held in Mount Carmel Monastery in Glasgow. For lack of a better alternative the name has been kept, though meetings were soon transferred to other venues. It all adds to the slightly arcane and obfuscated reputation that unfortunately attaches to the group.

PART TWO

Autobiographical

CHAPTER SEVEN

Early Years

I was born early in the morning of Wednesday 5 May 1926 in my maternal grandmother's house in Hamilton and baptised in St Mary's Church there on 9 May. My parents were Maurice and Lucy (McLaughlin) and I was the first born in a family of four.

A few months after I was born the family moved to the Burnbank district of Hamilton where I lived until I was sixteen. First Communion in St Cuthbert's church on 25 May 1933 and Confirmation on 22 September 1936 (by Archbishop Mackintosh or Bishop Graham, I forget which) and education at St Cuthbert's primary school (1931-1936), St Aloysius College, Glasgow (1936-1939), and then Our Lady's High School, Motherwell (1939-1942), sum up my early years.

Our family life was extremely happy, our home was truly Catholic and our parents loving and caring. I was a very reluctant schoolboy at the age of five but cannot remember whether I enjoyed primary school; I was not particularly happy at St Aloysius, happier at Our Lady's High School but I have never subscribed to the suspect assertion by my elders that schooldays are or were the happiest of my life. On the whole I was glad when they were over.

Sometimes I have wondered how the idea of priesthood developed in me. My parents made our home a place of faith and religious practice; going to Mass on Sundays and 'devotions' on Sunday evenings and some weekdays was routine. From perhaps the age of nine or ten, I went to Mass on weekdays when I could. Sometimes this involved a rush to be in time for school and I remember one occasion when I left my place immediately the priest disappeared into the sacristy; a devout old gentleman told me to kneel down again and finish my thanksgiving after Communion!

I was also an altar server for a few years. On my first debut, the 'head altar boy' told me to go and 'tim the thurible'. I guessed that the contraption he handed me must be the thurible but I hadn't the faintest idea what 'tim' meant and to my shame and embarrassment had to ask. Another memorably embarrassing experience was 'dropping the Missal', the very heavy book sliding off its stand to the floor as I struggled to carry it from the 'epistle side' to the 'gospel side'.

Much more embarrassing in retrospect (though it seemed to me a generous gesture at the time) occurred one Hallowe'en when I invited my fellow altar servers to come home with me because we had peanuts for them. On arrival, I indicated that they should stand in the street while I, from our front garden, threw handfuls of nuts to them! May the Lord – and they – forgive the little prig that I was.

I was in my second last year at secondary school and getting worried about 'what I wanted to be' when, one evening at confession, a priest whom I greatly admired in Burnbank (Fr Daniel B. White) asked me that very question. To my surprise but without hesitation, I said I thought I'd like to be a priest, so in the spring of 1942 the parish priest made formal application for me to the archdiocese of Glasgow (the establishment of the dioceses of Motherwell and Paisley did not take place until 1947). I was interviewed by a panel of formidable and venerable old priests who asked me to read a passage of the gospel in Latin; a few days later I was informed that I had been accepted as a student for the priesthood and that I would start my philosophy course at Blairs College, Aberdeen, that summer (August 1942).

CHAPTER EIGHT

Seminary

Having been told that I would be studying philosophy when I began my seminary training at the age of sixteen, I felt slightly embarrassed since I imagined that philosophers were not usually teenagers. Would we be sitting in deep leather armchairs, smoking pipes and solemnly discussing the problems of mankind and such like arcane matters? Teenage philosopher? Surely an oxymoron!

The reality was different. We were housed in part of Blairs College (which normally was a 'junior seminary' housing boys of secondary school age but, because of the wartime unavailability of Rome, Valladolid and Paris, had to make room for students in the first two years of their senior seminary course – the 'philosophers'). Our accommodation was worse than basic – tiny cubicles, the entrances being screened by an inadequate curtain, many without a window and all part of a large dormitory which doubled as our common room. We went to bed breathing air thick with cigarette smoke. And the food was equally sub-basic, predictable and monotonous. But it was wartime, we wanted to be priests, we accepted the conditions without complaint (this was the 1940s!) and I was very happy there, once recovered from initial homesickness.

By today's standards the regime was austere and exacting, with a strict discipline, a full daily programme of religious activities (Mass, morning, midday and night prayers, meditation, visit to the Blessed Sacrament, rosary, spiritual reading plus occasional extras). Academically there were classes (and exams) in various branches of Scholastic philosophy such as logic, metaphysics, psychology, cosmology and the history of philosophy:

quite demanding because so different from the subjects we had studied for our Highers.

Conditions for those in seminary training nowadays are necessarily very different and far less spartan and rigorous but in those days we were told if we felt hard done by, that we were lucky not to be students of sixty years previously.

And despite everything, they were an enjoyable two years at Blairs College with many happy memories, two of which I recall with special pleasure – my first (and only) opportunity to be 'master of ceremonies' at the weekly solemn High Mass (on Passion Sunday 1944), an honour I performed successfully and with great pride; and my completely unexpected victory in the final of the Blairs billiards tournament.

The Blairs song contained the brainwashing declaration that 'Joys of home how sweet so ever can't compare with those of Blairs'. A wicked exaggeration but I have happy memories of my two years there.

CHAPTER NINE

Military Service

I was eighteen in May 1944 and had to register for military service. In August that year my calling-up papers required me to report at Dreghorn Barracks, Edinburgh, for initial training.

If joining the seminary had been a culture shock, joining the army was a cultural cataclysm. And yet, at eighteen, I did not feel as traumatised as I would have done if I had been older. To contemplate the prospect now would terrify me and it is a consolation of old age to know that, even in dire necessity, it is unlikely that the country will ever need me again.

People have often said, 'I thought students for the priesthood were exempt from call-up', but it depended. Exemption was granted to those who had begun their studies before the outbreak of war in 1939 (thus if I had been at Blairs College for my secondary education) or if one's parish priest could declare that, before 1939, he knew of one's intention to apply to go to a seminary (mine couldn't and didn't).

Army life was a strange experience for me. I certainly didn't revel in it nor was I totally miserable. The first six weeks (at Dreghorn Barracks in Edinburgh) were pretty awful – a strict regime (as at Blairs) but with hardly any intellectual or spiritual content. Drill, route marches, rifle firing, grenade lobbing, bayonet practice (on hanging bags full of sand), kit inspections and barrack room conversation on topics and with vocabulary new and startling to my tender ears.

Having successfully avoided assignment to an infantry regiment by achieving a low score at rifle and Bren gun target practice (and thereby failing to win the sweepstake that was organised for us at sixpence each), I was enrolled in the Royal Army

Medical Corps and posted to its central barracks at Crookham in Hampshire. Life there was somewhat more civilised than at Dreghorn and it became even more so when, two months later, I was sent to Bristol to be trained in blood transfusion work. Much of our time there was taken up with cleaning used blood transfusion kits but, instead of barrack rooms, we were billeted in local civilian houses. Then to Moretonhampstead in Devon where a huge hotel on the edge of Dartmoor had been made into a military hospital; and later to Belfast where Campbell College had been similarly commandeered. In Belfast I watched the huge parade on the twelfth of July (1945) and was a frequent attendee at the weekly novena to Our Lady of Perpetual Succour at Clonard Redemptorist Monastery in the Falls Road district. It was only many years later, on a visit to Northern Ireland, that I realised the anomaly. My mention of having gone to the weekly novena – wearing a British Army uniform to do so – caused some astonishment. Those people (understandably after all their experience) did not normally associate a young British soldier with someone who attended novenas in the nationalist district and who wanted to be a priest.

In October 1945 (by this time it was two months after Japan's surrender) I was sent to India. From Liverpool the P&O liner (and wartime troopship) *Empress of Scotland* (formerly *Empress of Japan* but changed for obvious reasons) took us, with calls at Taranto, Port Said and Aden, to Bombay. The voyage lasted three weeks with many of us assigned hammocks on E deck (well below the waterline and in normal times for steerage baggage, I think – so hot, airless and uncomfortable that, when we got to warm nights, we slept on the open decks).

India was totally fascinating and on the whole I was happy. The ethos was generally relaxed and friendly. I got the chance of training and working as a radiographer and I became extremely interested in India – its history, its culture, its politics as it moved uneasily towards independence and partition.

After an initial few weeks in Deolali, north of Bombay (where we were warned about bubonic plague in the district

and inevitably I felt very ill for a few days and practically certain
that I had succumbed to the dreaded disease) I was sent to
Secunderabad (near Hyderabad) where I qualified as a radiographer and worked in a military hospital there for several
months. While there I got to know and admire two local priests,
both Italians – one was a parish priest as well as vicar general, elderly with a long white beard (inevitably called Santa Claus by
the soldiers) and the other a much younger priest with whom I
became very friendly. He was a zealous man who wanted to
identify so much with his parishioners that he tried various
methods, unsuccessfully, to dye his skin. Later I had postings to
Avadi (outside Madras), Bangalore and Bhopal.

I got to love India and its people – although my 21st birthday
(5 May 1947) passed unnoticed and unremarked by anyone and
I felt very lonely that day and greatly missing my family.

British troops were leaving India in preparation for the country's independence in August 1947. As the liner *Georgic* sailed
westward from Bombay I stood on deck looking back wistfully
and indeed sadly at the receding coastline of a beautiful and
wonderful land.

At the Suez Canal we were disembarked and taken to a camp
at a place called El Ballah, near the Canal, awaiting transfer to
Palestine – not a pleasant prospect at that time with Jewish
'terrorists' (or 'freedom fighters') targeting British soldiers who
garrisoned the country. Demobilisation was in progress and, although normally I would not have got out of the army for many
months, I applied for exceptional 'Class B' release to enable me
to resume my seminary studies.

While awaiting authority's decision (release or Palestine), I
used in the evening to go, if I could, to the Canal, sit on the stony
bank and dangle my feet in the cooling water. Occasionally a
ship would pass and, if it were going northwards, I would
watch it longingly.

After six or eight weeks in Egypt, word arrived. I was to be
granted Class B release. I sailed from Port Said to Liverpool, accommodated in the comfort and luxury of the *Franconias*'s sick

quarters, not because I was ill but because I and a few others were entrusted with caring for any who might be. No one was, so the voyage became a happy ending to my army career.

I have tried to give some idea of my feelings during my three years in the army rather than details of all that happened. In retrospect, I now think that the experience was beneficial. I don't know if it 'made a man of me' but it was a wonderful opportunity to get to know new places, new people – and myself. Moreover, even with my three years away from the seminary, I was still only 24 at ordination.

Did I reflect on the morality of World War II? Did my conscience bother me while in the army? Did I ever think of being a conscientious objector? The answer to all three questions is 'No'. If I had been older, the questions might have occurred to me, even bothered me. The Allies were opposed to powerful and unjust aggressors whose leaders were guilty of horrible crimes – but we were allies of the evil Soviet regime, we got involved with immoral and indiscriminate bombing of Germany, we collaborated in dropping atom bombs on Japanese cities.

I now doubt very much whether any war can be just – yet is there always and in every case an alternative? May God grant us the blessing of peace, guide the powerful to forswear all violence and protect the innocent, the weak and those without power.

CHAPTER TEN

Rome: Student for the Priesthood

'Demobbed' in the summer of 1947, I applied to return to my seminary training but I was in an uncertain frame of mind. Did I really want to be a priest? And if so, did I want to be a diocesan priest in Scotland or a missionary in India? However, I made my presence known to the diocesan authorities (still uncertain if I was doing the right thing), was assigned to St Peter's College, Cardross – but my destination was changed at the last minute to the Scots College, Rome. That change pleased me. I was excited at the prospect of living in Rome and I suppose that helped to resolve my indecision about my future.

Anyway, I found the college, both during the academic year in Rome and during three hot summer months in Marino (to the south of Rome and near Castel Gandolfo), a very happy place.

In the city we were living in those days right in the centre of things (in Via Quattro Fontane) and I took full advantage of getting to know the city, and especially its churches, very well. Things were still somewhat spartan only two years after the war but it was a marvellous and unexpected privilege to have been sent to Rome.

Papal occasions were awesome to this newcomer to the Eternal City. To be present in St Peter's when Pius XII was there – carried in on a throne borne on men's shoulders, surrounded by cardinals, monsignori, and I don't know what other great people, with trumpets filling the basilica with Grieg's Homage March and other solemn music, thousands of people reaching out to try to touch the Holy Father as he was carried past and screaming 'Viva il Papa' – I found it breathtaking and unforgettable.

Of course, there had to be a fly in the ointment in those happy years. It was study, classes at the Gregorian University and exams. I found it all quite difficult, perhaps because I had been away from books for three years, perhaps because I found classes in Latin (and as spoken by 'foreigners' and so rapidly) not at all easy to follow, and perhaps – no, I must admit, certainly – because I was lazy.

Anyway, somehow or other I got through the courses and the exams (four years of undergraduate theology and, after an interval of a year back in Scotland, a further two years as a post-graduate student for a doctorate in theology). One memorable academic triumph is worth recalling. Among the courses we had to do was Hebrew (admittedly at a very elementary level). As usual, I had left my study for the exam until the last minute. The night before the exam I realised I hadn't the faintest idea of the subject. In a panic I asked the resident student genius to explain a few things. He gave me an hour's tuition. The next morning I not only passed the Hebrew exam but got ten out of ten – 'summa cum laude'. If that proves anything, it is not something that should be spoken about – especially to those studying for exams. You may not be able to fool all the people all the time but you do seem to be able to fool some of the people some of the time.

The custom in those days was that the senior student due to begin his fourth year of theology was ordained at the end of his third year. The reason for this was that most of the students moved to the Scots summer villa in Marino and there were some days when no member of the staff was there. Hence the arrangement meant that there would always be a student who could celebrate Mass for the other students. I was the senior student in my year (by reason of being the only one) so I was ordained to the priesthood at the end of my third year in Rome: to be precise on Sunday 2 July 1950 in the chapel of the International Carmelite College in Rome, with about twenty other ordinands from various countries, by a Dutch Carmelite bishop who was a missionary in a very remote part of Brazil.

My parents, sisters, brother and a few relatives travelled by train from Scotland to be present at my ordination. They boarded at Pensione Maravilla on the top floor of a building in Via Napoleone III and it was there we had a celebratory meal after the ordination. The following day I 'said my first Mass' (with my father and brother serving) in the chapel of the Scots College villa in Marino.

Making the trip to Rome was a severe financial burden on my family but I was honoured by their presence and I believe they gladly made the sacrifice to be there (and to make their first visit to the Eternal City).

As seminarians, we didn't have much contact with Italians, at least 'ordinary' Italians. Some of us made friends with people from other colleges who were fellow students at the University. My special friend was Marcial Ramirez from Venezuela; we spoke in Latin because he knew no English and I had no Spanish. We lost contact for many years until I discovered, in the late 1980s, that he too had been made a bishop. The result was renewed contact by letter and phone, leading to exchange visits to each other's countries and homes.

Our social life in Rome was therefore fairly restricted and, to a large extent, was lived in our own Scots community in the college. But it was a happy place and the city was a wonderful experience. I was really sad when it came time to leave.

CHAPTER ELEVEN

Pale Young Curate

The archdiocese of Glasgow was divided in 1947 with the formation of the new dioceses of Motherwell and Paisley and (a change that would much later be of great personal interest to me) the northern part of Ayrshire which had belonged to the archdiocese since 1878 (from Largs to Stevenston and from Beith to Kilwinning) was given to the diocese of Galloway. Priests who were in the affected parishes at the time of the split became priests of the new dioceses (some priests who knew or guessed that change was coming made frantic efforts to be moved to the city of Glasgow 'before the music stopped' – a clerical amalgam of pass the parcel and musical chairs). Those of us who were still seminarians in 1948 were allocated to the diocese in which our home parish was situated. Hence I was assigned to the diocese of Motherwell as my home parish was Burnbank, Hamilton.

On each side of my two years' post-graduate course in Rome, I was given a year's parish work, first in St Bartholomew's, Coatbridge (1951-52) and then in St Bernadette's, Motherwell (1954 -55).

St Bartholomew's was a new parish. Fr Tom McGhie (parish priest) lived in a council house and had Sunday Mass in the local school. I was very green but Fr McGhie was a kind mentor. Apart from the obvious duties of a priest, he taught me many useful activities – how to play pontoon (I was apathetic and therefore pathetic), how to visit parishioners (keep your hat on for hygienic reasons and, if you felt that that was rude, lay your hat upside down on wood, not upholstery), how to eat a large meal in ten minutes so as to get to Celtic Park in time.

I tried my hand at a boys' club (abject failure – see elsewhere for a full account) and at 'instructing a convert' (as we called it in those days). The poor lady must have been totally bored with my inadequate efforts to 'instruct' her which ended, to her astonishment and alarm, with her baptism over the bath in our council house toilet. The recollection still gives me frissons of embarrassment.

St Bernadette's in Motherwell was also a new parish, but we had a church and an adequate house for us three priests (plus housekeeper and maid, both resident). The problem was that there was over a mile between the house and church. That was an incentive for me to learn to drive. By the way, I think that the driving test(s) can well stand comparison with any other of life's ordeals and emerge near the top.

Fr Peter Sexton was what I suppose would be described as an old-fashioned Irish parish priest. He was a character, eccentric, respected, a mixture of homespun philosophy and Shakespearean erudition. He had his own solution to the Easter Vigil liturgy, in those days celebrated in an empty church on Holy Saturday morning. Since we were three priests, I was sent to the back of the church to read the Prophecies (i.e. Old Testament readings), my fellow-curate went to the baptistery to 'do' the Exsultet, the blessing of the paschal candle and the font (with litany) while he 'got on with the Mass at the altar'. It certainly shortened the Easter Vigil. I wonder if similar ingenuity is in use anywhere today!

CHAPTER TWELVE

Cardross: Seminary Lecturer

Not unexpectedly (because of my postgraduate spell in Rome) I was appointed to the teaching staff at St Peter's College, Cardross (which took students from Glasgow, Motherwell and Paisley) in 1955.

Also not unexpectedly, having specialised in theology, I was sent to teach philosophy, or more accurately, certain subjects in the philosophy course. Formal logic, metaphysics and the history of ancient and medieval philosophy were my assigned subjects. Pedagogical methods were left more or less entirely to oneself while as far as subject matter was concerned I had, it is true, done a philosophy course (as a student in Blairs College) in 1942-44 but had not looked at the matter since then. So it was a case of buying the books, keeping a few pages ahead of the students and hoping nervously for the best.

I started my lecturing career inauspiciously. Seeking to be thorough, I decided, before embarking on the history of early Greek philosophy, to devote twenty minutes or so each to the history of the even earlier philosophies of China and Egypt. As examples of the former, my book mentioned Confucianism and Tao-ism so I remarked that Tao-ism still had its followers as there was a Tao institute in Glasgow. One of the students raised his hand to tell me, publicly, that the Tao Centre was 'for the removal of surplus hair'.

It was a humbling start to my lecturing career – like being ordered off after scoring an own goal on your home debut – but it taught me a lesson difficult to forget. Pride certainly went before a fall on that occasion. And a little knowledge is a dangerous thing.

After five generally happy years in the philosophy section (Darleith) of St Peter's College – during which I bought my first car for £30 (second hand, no heater, no radio, little orange lateral indicators which sometimes worked), I was transferred to the senior of the two houses (Kilmahew) to teach theology. This was more familiar ground and I was asked to teach the second, third and fourth years of theology as a cycle course. Perhaps the general atmosphere in Kilmahew was not as relaxed and 'homely' as Darleith but I was happier with the subjects I had to teach.

After all these years it is too easy to be critical of St Peter's College and especially Kilmahew in the years from 1960 to 1965. But I think the leadership was weak, discipline was lax and a proper sense of community was missing. Moreover the roles of the three bishops (Archbishop Campbell, Bishop Scanlan and Bishop Black) were unclear, their relationship among themselves apparently not close and their attitude towards the seminary ambiguous.

The sixties were generally a time of change, of turmoil, of student revolt, of crisis of authority – and it would have been naïve to imagine that a seminary be uninfluenced and exempt. Besides, the construction of the new building had begun alongside the Kilmahew nineteenth-century house and, among us from the start, the whole business was a source of concern and dismay. The design and architecture of the new building may have impressed architects and others who were not going to live and work in it but to us it was clearly impractical and unsuitable. For example, it was evident that, as a result of the Second Vatican Council, the style of liturgical celebration was about to change but the arrangements of the new building did not cater for that.

I remember that, at one stage, the teaching staff at Cardross became so worried at the design and proposed arrangements of the building that, although we had never been consulted about the project, the senior priest among us sought to bring our views to the Glasgow archdiocesan authorities. I don't remember whether he was granted a hearing or not, but no heed was paid to our concerns or suggestions.

So they weren't altogether easy, happy days in my later years in Cardross. One bitter incident remains vivid in my memory. It was the time of student riots and the struggle for desegregation in the United States. One morning, our students had been refused a day off which they wanted and, as I waited to go into the lecture hall to give a class, they began to sing loudly 'We shall overcome'. In retrospect, the incident was trivial and somewhat ludicrous, but it was serious for us then and menacing. I was very shaken. It was not a pleasant experience.

One day in 1965, before the summer holidays, I received a letter from the newly-ordained Bishop of Motherwell, Bishop Frank Thomson. I expected it to be a reply to my request for a photograph and message from him for our college magazine but, to my utter astonishment, it told me that the Bishops' Conference had appointed me to be rector of the Royal Scots College in Spain. Total surprise and shock – I had hardly adverted to the fact of the vacancy in Valladolid and certainly had not even dreamed of being asked to fill it. The letter bluntly added, 'Your ignorance of Spanish will not be accepted as grounds for refusal. You will just have to learn the language.'

CHAPTER THIRTEEN

Valladolid: Seminary Rector

The thought of going to Spain and of being rector of the Royal Scots College seemed very, very strange to me and exciting also. I wasn't a reluctant appointee but intrigued at the prospect of a new job in a country new to me – and I felt very honoured to have been chosen.

When you start a new job, you are not aware of all the duties that await you – and that was true for me in July 1965. But obviously there was the language and my ignorance of it. True, among the community of priests and students we spoke English – but we had constant contact with Spaniards. I felt like Zechariah, John the Baptist's father, but his speech was fully restored after nine months. I was gradually learning some Spanish right from the start (for example, when meeting someone for the first time, you can say *'mucho gusto'* or *'encantado'*) but it was a struggle, first to understand what people were saying, then to answer them intelligently. Gradually my vocabulary increased, my grammar improved and I gained confidence. If I were now asked for advice for someone in my plight it would be twofold: don't be afraid to make mistakes and never decide you are good enough!

It wasn't long before I discovered that being rector of the Royal Scots College was more than being in charge of the students (usually about twenty , all training to be priests in Scottish dioceses). That was difficult enough, especially in the worldwide turmoil of the late 60s, with student riots, crisis in authority etc. But I also had to deal with the college domestic staff, with tradesmen and workmen and local officialdom. The college owned a large estate called Canterac in another part of

Valladolid, a summer house, a pine wood and extensive vine-
yards in Boecillo (ten miles south of Valladolid, on the River
Duero), and property in Madrid. It had to be a very steep learning curve but I was helped, supported and consoled by the two
other staff members, already there when I arrived and indeed
former students, Fr (now Bishop) Ian Murray and Fr (now Mgr)
Jack Sheridan.

Shortly after I arrived in Spain, the college got involved in
court action against a man who had done a lot of paid work for
the college and had become friendly with my predecessor. The
problem was to dislodge him from a portion of our Canterac estate which he had occupied (illegally, we maintained). It was a
very disagreeable business, employing lawyers and taking our
dispute through the courts. We lost the criminal case so were advised to take civil action – which we also lost. I felt disheartened
and cynical. We were sure that justice had been denied us but
we lost the land and had to meet the cost of our lawyers' fees.

My main duty as rector was, of course, to look after the students. They received most of their classes in the local diocesan
seminary and, later, in an Augustinian Institute affiliated to the
University of Comillas. But we gave additional classes in the college and were responsible for the students' human, spiritual and
pastoral development as well as generally being responsible for
their safety, welfare, health and happiness. End of term assess-
ments had to be made, progress reports on each student sent to
his bishop in Scotland and, a task I greatly disliked, having
occasionally from time to time to dismiss a student or recom-
mend to his bishop that he be withdrawn. In such cases, I was
only too well aware of the responsibility I had – and indeed the
power – to make a decision of such great importance for the student himself and for his diocese. In the majority of occasions
when a student left, of course, it was of his own volition. That
was a preferable and better way.

Attending the Bishops' Conference once a year and giving a
report was another task (worse in anticipation than in reality). I
used to remind bishops that we needed students and would be

grateful for new recruits to the community; one year I appealed especially for a goalkeeper who could play the organ. One bishop obliged. The new man could do both (just) but unfortunately was not called to be a priest.

The college summer house at Boecillo was a great favourite of mine. In my day some of the students went home for the summer but most went to Boecillo. So did I (since I went to Scotland each spring and autumn). They were happy times – an old 1795 large solid building (used by Wellington during the Peninsular War), away from the city, in a commanding situation with extensive views, the river Duero nearby for swimming, priests visiting from Scotland, a real sense of community (in Spanish *'convivencia'* which I once saw unfortunately translated as 'cohabitation'). Our summer house was for relaxation and tranquillity except, for example, when we erected scaffolding round the whole building and all of us worked together to restore the walls to perfect whiteness, painting them with quicklime. On another occasion I was foolhardy enough to drive a tractor with trailer attached, lost control and was very lucky not to capsize or collide as we careered down a short but steep hill. There were students on the trailer, some of whom received cuts and scrapes as they leapt off in panic.

In the years until 1971, much of my spare time was occupied by preparing and writing *The Scots College in Spain*, a history of the college from its foundation in Madrid in 1627. The college had been transferred to Valladolid in 1771 and, to celebrate the bicentenary of that event, the book was published. Moreover, for a period of three days at the end of May and the beginning of June 1971, the college hosted a number of events (Masses, meals, receptions) for the Scottish bishops, many former students now priests in Scotland and a great collection of Spanish people, some of them dignitaries, some with an official connection to the college and others simply friends. They were successful and memorable days despite the fact that we were being picketed by people who lived near our Canterac estate and who thought we were selling it for housing. Groups of them were standing in the street outside the college, holding placards. Cardinal Gray gave them his blessing and a cheery wave, thinking that they had come to express their delight and congratulations on the occasion of the bicentenary.

My being sent to Valladolid, such an unexpected appointment, turned out to be very much to my liking. There were difficult moments but I was extremely happy in Spain. However, after nine years I felt it was time for me to ask the bishops to let me return to Scotland. The college needed a change and I didn't want to be in Spain so long that I would not be glad to resume parish work in Scotland. So, nine years to the day from my arrival, on 2 July 1974, I bade the college, the community and Spain a sad, indeed tearful, *Adiós*.

The question has often been asked: why have a college or seminary in Spain? Only through having experienced life there can one answer the question adequately but let me list some reasons: the college (and its assets) cannot easily be sold or funds removed from Spain; the college is well endowed so that the cost to a diocese of having a student there is a small fraction of the cost in the other seminaries; the Spanish pontifical universities offer an excellent academic formation; it is a very broadening and enriching experience to live abroad for a time; to learn at first hand the history, culture and language of Spain is an invaluable advantage in today's world; Scots seminarians in Spain can and do have lots of contacts outside the college; the students really enjoy being in Spain and remember it with great affection; finally the priests educated in Spain are second to none, are they not?

At present and due to the dearth of seminarians, the Royal Scots College (located in Salamanca since 1988) has no students doing their full undergraduate course before priesthood. The college is still very much in use for the ongoing formation of bishops, priests and deacons as well as providing a valuable resource, in a variety of ways, for the Catholics of Scotland. Nevertheless, my fervent hope is that, once again, and soon, the college may resume its work as a fully active seminary, training priests for Scotland. Then we shall all be the beneficiaries.

CHAPTER FOURTEEN

East Kilbride

Our Lady of Lourdes parish, East Kilbride, to which Bishop Thomson appointed me as parish priest in August 1974 is large, completely post-World War II and welcoming. I took to it very easily and readily, despite my parish experience being limited and twenty years out of date. I got great support and understanding from the other two priests and from the people. And of course, settling into East Kilbride was not as challenging as it had been in Valladolid.

I was very happy as a parish priest, perhaps because it was a good time: long enough after the Second Vatican Council to be introducing 'new' insights from its teaching on the nature of the church, on liturgy, on ecumenism etc. But it would have been quite wrong to abandon all previous religious practices and ideas.

This sat very comfortably with me and while we were introducing a parish pastoral council, a more participative liturgy and more frequent contact with Christians from other churches and traditions, we still had Rosary and Benediction, Holy Hours, visits to parishioners in their homes and regular visiting of the hospital and the schools.

As I look back on those seven years in East Kilbride (1974-1981), there are certain aspects of life there that I remember with particular appreciation.

One was the happiness of 'collaborative ministry', sharing the work with parishioners through discussion, planning and carrying out various activities. It was good not to be solely responsible, to help people become aware that, through baptism, they were as much the church as the priests were and that they were called to be active, to use the gifts the Holy Spirit had given them. Not everyone responded but it was heart warming that so many did.

Another source of happiness for me was the parish charismatic prayer group that met each Thursday evening. We had our struggles to keep it going in its early days but then it did truly flourish and, for many of us, was a real grace as we learned to pray communally, spontaneously and without embarrassment. The scriptures became more familiar and meaningful, hymns became prayers, and we became, in grace, closer to God and to each other. The Holy Spirit was present and active in our midst.

Nor do I forget the feeling I gradually experienced in the parish of being understood, accepted and appreciated. In a seminary I think that the students tend to take one for granted or, at least, are not good at showing appreciation or expressing gratitude. So it was really affirming to be thanked and appreciated. In return, I became able, indeed sought, to be seen as a human being, imperfect and vulnerable, with feelings and emotions, making mistakes, grateful for being allowed to grow in friendship. It can be difficult for parishioners to achieve the right attitude towards their priest. He must be seen as having a ministry different from lay people and being respected for that, but also allowed and enabled to be a human being who needs relationships, who needs to love and be loved. Our Lady of Lourdes parish meant that for me.

PART THREE

Present Thoughts and Past Experience

CHAPTER FIFTEEN

Travel

Being a bishop increased my opportunities for travel to far off lands. It gave some justification to the riddle: 'What is the difference between God and a bishop?' 'God is everywhere but a bishop is everywhere except in his own diocese.' I always enjoyed the overseas trips and found them most interesting. So I am happy to recall some memories of them. An added bonus was that, on many occasions, the air fare was not my responsibility.

Before I became a bishop in 1981 and for a few years thereafter, I was secretary to the Bishops' Conference of Scotland and during my term of office the custom of an annual meeting of the secretaries of European Bishops' Conferences was begun. That provided trips to Bruges, Malta and Budapest. In Hungary we were accommodated in a Redemptorist house on the Danube, a few miles west of the capital. Hungary was still in the Soviet bloc and, when we had Mass during the meeting, the man in the house next door put on his radio as loud as he could, presumably to annoy us. On the Sunday, however, we had a splendid celebration of Mass in Budapest cathedral, with the archbishop as principal celebrant, organ, choir, candles, incense and the first 'altar girls' I had ever seen. Two other Hungarian memories – the reckless speed of the taxis especially when overtaking on bends; and the genial Redemptorist superior who insisted on our having a glass of plum brandy each morning before breakfast.

At one of the European secretaries' meetings, there was an announcement that the Federation of Asian Bishops would like a European representative to attend their forthcoming meeting. As I, by then, fulfilled the two conditions (a bishop who spoke

English) I found myself in Tokyo for the meeting. My memory of that city is its size, its bewildering bustle and the archbishop's house where I was given warm hospitality despite having committed an initial solecism of not having changed my outdoor shoes to one of the pairs of slippers at the entrance.

I also managed to spend a few days in Kyoto, the old capital of Japan with many religious shrines and temples and where the local bishop took me to have a private and traditional meal of about ten (small) courses with a spoon courteously provided for me in addition to chopsticks. A further bonus was a day (by 'bullet train') in Hiroshima where the devastation caused by the 1945 atom bomb is still poignantly 'preserved' as an affront, a reproach and a plea to humankind.

Invitations to speak at charismatic meetings took me to Australia, Ireland, Malta, the Czech Republic as well as to Canada (Winnipeg in Manitoba and Kamloops in British Columbia – it should have been Vancouver but the archbishop refused permission).

Appointment as the Scottish representative on the Episcopal Board of the International Commission on English in the Liturgy took me quite frequently to Washington DC. For that journey my preferred route was via Reykjavik, not only because it was more pleasant than via London but also because the airline seemed very appropriate for my purposes : ICELandair. I remember one occasion when we left Iceland for Washington after dusk and, as we flew across the ocean, I saw the sun rise in the west.

Perhaps most interesting of all was travel in connection with and deriving from my membership of the Catholic Institute for International Relations, an organisation based in London and working for human rights and progress in the developing world. I was invited in 1984 to become a vice-president because the Institute wanted greater Scottish involvement and because I could speak Spanish, an advantage since much of the work concerns Latin America.

My CIIR connection has brought me many visits to Central

America, especially El Salvador and Guatemala. (My involvement with those countries deserves a fuller account which is to be found in later chapters.) I hope that I can continue to visit Central America because I now have some good friends there but I found, on my latest trip there in October 2004, that some of the hardships and discomforts of life there were becoming more difficult to accept than they used to be.

Other contacts (and my knowledge of Spanish) have afforded opportunities to visit South America on several occasions. Venezuela (where I went to meet a bishop who had been a fellow-student in Rome in the late 1940s), Chile (I had been invited to be a member of a delegation when the people there voted against General Augusto Pinochet in a national plebiscite), Ecuador (to visit Scottish priests working there) and Colombia (as a member of a Pax Christi delegation from the Netherlands – fascinating, memorable but not for the faint-hearted).

I remember with pleasure two trips I made and without any official purpose. One was to Zimbabwe (with a priest colleague) to visit Mgr Peter Magee, the first priest that I ordained (on 2 July 1981) and, at the time of our visit, the secretary in the Nunciature in Harare. We managed to travel extensively in various parts of the country, meeting many people including, in Bulawayo, Fr Pius Ncube, now the courageous archbishop of that city, and seeing some wonderful sights, above all Victoria Falls.

The other trip was to India, nearly fifty years after my time there as a soldier. I managed to visit two cities, Delhi and Agra, that I had not visited before but perhaps the highlight was to visit places where I had been stationed while I was in the army. I particularly remember going to the very barrack room near Secunderabad where I had spent some months in 1946. It was a very strange feeling to stand on the spot where my bed and belongings (and I) had been so many years before and so many miles from home and to realise that that young man had been me, unaware of all that was to befall me. An uncanny experience.

CHAPTER SIXTEEN

Chaplain to the Canaries

One raw December afternoon in the early 1960sI walked down Fish Street Hill in London past Billingsgate Market and then, for the first time in my life, stepped on to Spanish territory. The particular piece of Spain on which I trod was the Bilbao-registered ship, *Monte Urquiola*, which maintains (or maintained) a fortnightly service between London and the Canary Islands, carrying bananas, tomatoes and people. The ministrations of a Catholic chaplain were deemed necessary, not for any of these three categories (apparently only the occasional English Catholic had the necessary leisure or inclination to winter in Tenerife), but for the crew who, being Spanish, were, of course, all Catholics.

Those were happy days as we sped sunwards at twelve knots – and memorable too, since we enjoyed the roughest weather anyone could remember. Lunch on New Year's Day was taken in, or at least on, bed – a cup of weak tea and a water biscuit. But not every day was as bad and I recall having had some meals in the dining room. There was the occasion, for example, when, during afternoon tea, one lady was a little late in clutching the edge of the table and with a cry of 'My God!' was tipped off her chair and slid ungracefully across the room and into the far corner, followed closely by her chair and a large amount of the ship's crockery.

However, I restrict myself to recalling some incidents of a more strictly religious character. On the Sunday, I was informed that I would be saying two Masses, one at an early hour for the ordinary seamen and another at ten for the officers. The weekday Mass had not been exactly a sell-out, but it was reasonable enough to have two Masses on Sunday since a ship sailing the high *(sic)* seas with every member of the crew attending Mass at the same time is somewhat unusual and even perilous. It was disappointing to have, as one's congregation at the first Mass, the altar server (of whom more later) and about six seamen, lurking sheepishly in the further corners of the room.

For the second Mass, I was ready and vested at ten, but the turnout was equally sparse. I thought I'd wait a few minutes just in case any more came, but by five past the situation was unchanged. So I began Mass. During the first reading, the door opened and in trooped the captain, followed, to a man, by all the other officers. Perhaps there is some unwritten law of the Spanish main that ordinary seamen don't attend Mass but that officers do. My feeling, afterwards, that at least the latter did come to Mass even if they had not quite been on time – this smug reflection – was devastatingly dispelled when it was communicated to me that the 10am Mass began only when the officers had arrived and that the captain was very displeased at my non-compliance with the rule.

The ship's barman was called Jesús and, perhaps for that reason, had been the Mass server for a long time. But recently he had acquired a young assistant, Ramón, who had once been a seminarian for three weeks and to him had naturally been delegated the liturgical duties. Ramón took me under his wing at once and felt it incumbent upon himself to undertake an apostolate of liturgical pedagogy. In other words, he dedicated himself to teaching me, during Mass each morning, how to celebrate it properly. (Those were pre-Vatican II days, by the way.)

Apparently he felt that I needed speeding up with the prayers at the foot of the altar, since he would give the answer to the verse that I had been hoping to say next; this is good training in patience and concentration – try it sometime. He would disappear discreetly for considerable periods during Mass to see, I think, if I could manage on my own for a while. Each morning he presented me with the water cruet first so that he could then correct my attempt to say 'wine' in Spanish and teach me to pronounce the word properly; when he considered that I had at least made a praiseworthy effort, he would hand over the wine cruet with a word of congratulation. He was a most helpful youth who gave me all the assistance in his power. In those days at the end of Mass one had to say, *'Benedicat vos omnipotens Deus'* facing the altar and then turn round to finish the blessing. Ramón used to allow me to say the first four words but, by the time I had turned round, he had already piously intoned *'Pater et Filius et Spiritus Sanctus'* to which I responded a dutiful if sheepish *'Amen'*. An estimable youth. I wonder where he is now. A leading figure in Catholic action, perhaps. Or a bishop.

The passengers treated me with respect, under the impression that I was a permanent member of the crew. 'How long do you reckon this storm will last, padre?' 'Does this ship always roll as much as this?' There was also a certain reserve, increased perhaps by the fact that the passengers were English as well as non-Catholic. I recall with affection, however, one very pleasant, elderly Englishman who, from time to time in the intervals between dreadful bouts of seasickness, would emerge from his cabin. He was a Church of England clergyman, a gentle soul, who was going to Tenerife for a few months for the sake of his health. On the Saturday afternoon he asked me whether I thought it would be a good idea if he were to hold a Holy Communion service the following morning for the benefit of those passengers who were interested. I said it was an excellent idea and then he disclosed that he had none of the wherewithal and wondered would I be willing to co-operate. I felt that I could hardly lend him the chalice and paten for which he asked, nor allow him to use the altar. I explained that these objects were consecrated and set apart so that even Catholics were forbidden to use them for anything except Mass. He was so understanding that I thought no harm would be done by giving him some hosts and wine and, putting our heads together, we decided that a coffee table, a wineglass and a small plate, while not ideal, would be fairly acceptable to the Lord in the special circumstances. Finally, he asked if nine o'clock the following day would be suitable, so as not to be in the way at the time of my Masses.

So all was arranged and off he went to let the captain know, so that the matter might be announced to the passengers. He returned a few minutes later, utterly crestfallen. He had explained all the arrangements to the captain, who then informed him that we were on a Spanish ship and that therefore he would not permit any non-Catholic religious rites. And that was that.

My friend, by this time thoroughly demoralised, asked if I thought there would be any objection to his coming to Mass, as otherwise he would not be present at any act of worship. I assured him that, as far as I was concerned, there was no objection. And so next morning, he was a member of the congregation at the ten o'clock Mass, taking his place at ten minutes to ten.

CHAPTER SEVENTEEN

The Delights of Turkish Travel

[I wrote this essay in 1963. Travel in Turkey nowadays must be different and so the article has acquired a 'period-piece' quality]

'Fly!' urged the travel agent, 'It's the only way to get around this country.' A priest friend and I were in Istanbul, planning a tour of Asia Minor, Turkey-in-Asia. Had we taken the travel agent's advice, we should have deprived ourselves of not the least of the delights which Turkey offers the visitor. Turkish surface transport may not be the last word in luxury but is certainly an experience that the conscientious tourist should not try to avoid.

Most popular for long distance travel are the buses. You go along to the local bus depot a day or two beforehand to book a seat. Scores of bus lines operate out of the larger cities with perhaps two or three specialising in each route. The buses may, in many cases, be ancient lurching juggernauts but the companies all have the word 'Jet' incorporated in their name. 'Express' would presumably denote a company still using horse-buses. Before departure time, you present yourself at the bus stance to have your cases securely but crudely roped on the roof and to claim your seat – and the journey begins. One's fellow travellers are a cross-section of the Turkish people , young and old, comfortable and poor, modern and old-fashioned. Nor is it long before a foreigner has attracted the interest of at least one or two of them. Halting conversation is begun and you are offered a share in the food-hampers that nearly everyone seems to have – cherries, some figs or tomatoes. It is at such moments that you are faced with the dilemma of remaining true to the rule of never eating unwashed, unpeeled fruit and so seeming ungrateful or just going ahead and immediately experiencing all sorts of aches and pains that can only presage cholera or typhoid, if not both. Much better if your new-found acquaintances produce oranges, peaches or even a water-melon.

The bus driver is much more important than in our own country. Apart from his obvious duties and responsibilities, it is he who decides when and where the stops will be made, for how long they will last, whether the passengers will be allowed off or whether they will remain on the bus, to be ministered to by an invasion of vendors of *ayran* (the cool refreshing drink of diluted yoghurt that is almost a national beverage). He also decides whether the bus radio will be turned on and just how deafening the music will be; and whether every other road-user that passes or is passed will be treated to several blasts of the ear-shattering horn. These are important decisions when you are condemned to spending all day in a bus, in a temperature approaching 100 degrees and when your nerves tend, after a little, to become ever so slightly frayed at the edges.

However, I must be fair. No matter its length, the driver has to do the full journey on his own, without benefit of a relief driver. I recall a magnificent specimen of Turkish manhood – bullet-headed, moustachioed with whiskers more like buffalo horns than handlebars, who drove his bus from Izmir to Adana, 600-700 miles, from 1pm until 10am the following morning.

After some hours on the bus, of course, a sticky lethargy tends to take over and you hardly bother to notice the string of camels by the roadside or to register that the village with the unpronounceable name through which the bus is passing was once Nicomedia or Thyatira or Laodicea or some other place mentioned in the New Testament. Stretches of ruts and potholes are much more effective for jolting you back to full consciousness, but such are not very frequent, most of the roads, even if only with a gravel surface, being fairly smooth.

One drawback in bus travel is the difficulty you have in discovering the estimated time of arrival. Timetables seem unavailable, the booking agent who hopes to sell you a ticket is very optimistic and reassuring but as the journey gets under way the rumours that circulate become gloomier and gloomier. The best plan is to be mentally detached from such worries and anxieties. The information is largely irrelevant in such an easy-going country as Turkey and, besides, the fare is less than £1 for 400 miles.

The railways issue timetables of course, but their value is rather curtailed when you realise that (due to bus competition and cheapness) many trains do not run daily and that the train at the time most suitable for your needs runs on 'Pazartesi and Cuma only' (or is it 'excepted'?). The safest plan in this case would seem to be to present yourself at the station at the correct time each day and eventually, one day, the train is bound to appear. There are some fast diesel services but the steam trains have much more character. They go slowly enough to allow peasants in the fields to give a friendly wave to the travellers, if not actually to jog along beside them.

I recall an all-day journey from Konya (Iconium in the New Testament) to Tarsus. The scenery was remarkable, often breathtaking, as we crossed the barren central plateau of Anatolia, passed through the towering mountains of the Taurus range and dropped down through the narrow defiles of the Cilician Gates to the semi-tropical maritime plain of southern Turkey. Despite the magnificence, the journey was just as memorable on account of our compartment co-passengers – the little old man, for example, sitting quietly in a corner who suddenly slid his feet out of his shoes, drew his legs up under him, put a prayer cap on his head, turned towards Mecca and unconcernedly went through his evening prayer ritual. Then there were the three boys who had been on the train since the previous day but had sought us out in the milling crowds to let us know that they had a spare seat and would crush up to make a second seat available. They were friendly and full of fun. They soon produced a pack of cards and were delighted to be taught some games that we knew. By the end of the journey, with the aid of a little good-natured cheating, they could beat us every time. And let any anthropologist beware of oversimplification if he decides to write a

thesis on the card games indigenous to the remote areas of
south-east Asia Minor. I am afraid we have contaminated the
evidence and complicated his task.

Shorter journeys can be made by private taxi, if you are an
American or a former *pasha*. Everyone else uses a *dolmus*, an
admirable institution for cheap and convenient movement between two points. A *dolmus* is a shared-taxi and in the bigger
cities this form of conveyance does a constant trade. You simply
go to a square or other central point and help to fill up the *dolmus*
whose destination is where you want to go. In a few moments,
the car is full and off you go – only a little dearer than the city
bus, yet much quicker and more comfortable. *Dolmuses* also
make longer trips out of town. In these cases the *dolmus* is often a
minibus with room for about eight passengers and you may
have to wait for a little longer before the vehicle is full. For example, *dolmuses* regularly ply between Izmir and the ruins of
Ephesus, 50 miles to the south, take their passengers round the
various places of interest there and bring them back to Izmir in
the evening. And they are frequently used as land ferries to the
beaches, from Istanbul to the Black Sea, for instance, or from
Mersin to the ruins-cum-beach at Soli where the inhabitants
once spoke such execrable Greek that they gave the world a new
word – solecism.

Perhaps the most attractive of all Turkish transport, however,
is the horse-cab. Some of the holiday islands in the Sea of
Marmara have banned all internal combustion engines from
their streets and a gentle ride along them by horse-cab, past pine
woods and summer villas, is a balm to the nerves after the clam-
our and crowds of Istanbul. But when you get to some of the
towns of Asia Minor, it is to discover that the horse-cab is not
there as a tourist attraction but that it is the only form of transport in the place. No doubt there are compensations for being so
far behind the times but please do not suggest freedom from
breakdowns as one such compensation . At Mersin, on the south
coast, the railway station is a mile from town and so a cab is a necessity. We had just passed one of the only two possible hotels in

the town, having rejected the entreaties of its owner to put up there, when a wheel rib came off our cab; in full view of the disappointed hotel owner we had to dismount and, carrying our cases, walk to the other hotel. Our 'humiliation' was not yet complete: no accommodation available there and so nothing for it but a sheepish return to the hotel we had previously spurned and a servile request to be forgiven.

Although our journeying in Turkey had been accomplished without leaving the ground, fate (in the form of a Syrian refusal to grant us visas) decreed that we should have to take to the air to leave the country and continue our journey southwards. And so it was that we alighted from a *dolmus* at the end of the side road in which the entrance to Adana airport is. Not a taxi or cab was in sight and there was nothing for it but to cover the half mile on foot and carrying our own luggage – hardly the way in which the best people arrive at airports. Our self-esteem was restored, however, by a glance at our plane tickets for we were travelling by the national airline Turk Hava Yollari and there, on the cover of our tickets, were the very charming and flattering words 'THY Airline'.

CHAPTER EIGHTEEN

Faith

Life is God's first gift to us and then consequently God gives us those gifts which are needed for life's preservation and development, especially the gift of loving parents.

As Catholics we also thank God for the special and additional gifts that are sometimes called supernatural – and basic among these is faith.

To the question 'What is faith?' the *Catechism of Christian Doctrine* which we used when I was at school answered that 'Faith is a supernatural gift of God that enables us to believe without doubting whatever God has revealed.'

The Catechism of the Catholic Church (1992) is similar but longer: 'Faith is the theological virtue by which we believe in God and believe all that he has said and revealed to us and that Holy Church proposes for our belief, because he is truth itself.' (#1814)

These descriptions are fine as far as they go, but they do not go very far. They intend to tell us what faith is, they analyse its essence, but questions remain. Are the two definitions not in danger of begging the question by using the word 'believe'? What does that word mean? And I am sure that most of us seek not to have a definition of faith, but to have faith. And by that I do not mean the body of teaching that is sometimes called 'the faith' (as in 'We have the true faith') but a total conviction of the truth of what God reveals to us (through Jesus and the church). Am I totally convinced – and on the grounds of God's truthfulness and trustworthiness, and not only on human motives, either my own or others?

These are vitally important matters obviously. Am I convinced that God exists? Am I convinced that there is a life after death? Eternal life with God?

In the seminary during our philosophy course we were taught the 'Five Ways' as laid out by St Thomas Aquinas – five ways of proving by reason that there is (or rather must be) a God. They are metaphysical proofs and convince me; in summary, that you cannot have even an infinite number of caused causes – there has also to be a first cause, a being that is not dependent on another for its existence. There are, in addition, the powerful arguments for God's existence based on the order, complexity, beauty of the universe and its components – all of which cannot have happened by chance but demand a supreme intelligence.

But let us not forget that faith is a gift of God to us and, though we can use our reasoning to develop it and discover its implications, its source is not ourselves or our powers of reasoning.

One could continue to ask questions and some of them still challenge us as well as theologians. For example, does God offer the gift of faith to every human being (because if not, that would seem unjust)? If Catholic Christianity possesses the truth about God etc., where does that leave others? Do Jews and Muslims not have the same utter conviction of faith that we should have, but whose tenets contradict some Christian beliefs? But I digress and prefer to leave such questions to better theologians than me.

God gives us faith – and God will strengthen that gift if I pray. I often think of the incident in the gospel and identify with the man who said to Jesus, 'Lord, I believe. Help my unbelief.'

And God does just that. Personally, I find my faith strengthened when I am with others and worshipping in particularly moving circumstances – on a pilgrimage, at an ordination or funeral, when celebrating the sacrament of reconciliation, at a charismatic event. We need Tabor occasions to restore and strengthen our faith on the journey through life to death, to reassure us that there is a beyond and that God awaits us there.

One personal memory will always be vivid with me. It was in September 1967 and I had been called home from Spain because

my father was dying. Although he was very weak I was able to
spend a lot of time with him. He liked when I said Night Prayer
aloud from the Breviary. One psalm spoke of death and the
grave – and I broke down and wept. He called me over to his
bed, to embrace me and console me and to tell me that he had no
fear of death since he was, and would be, in God's hands. At that
moment, I experienced a renewal of faith, an awareness that, no
matter what doubts might tempt me in the future, I had been
totally convinced of God's loving providence. The memory of
that experience sustains me as a very personal support to the
faith I received at baptism.

CHAPTER NINETEEN

Praying

Praying is not easy. At least, for me, it isn't. Perhaps that statement needs to be qualified. It is easy enough to say prayers, and perhaps also it should be added that the near inevitability of distractions while saying prayers does not destroy their value. But when I say that praying is difficult I mean the quality and amount of time I am willing to give, the priority that praying has in my life, the faith which I bring to prayer, the daily commitment, the perseverance ...

It is humbling when people presume that a priest, indeed a bishop, is good at praying, that he knows the secret that they don't know, that he is an expert because he is ordained. I feel like saying 'It's not so', but such a disclaimer is taken for humility and only increases the fiction.

Anyway, having got that off my chest, let me offer some thoughts, experiences and preferences on prayer. (For the present, I prescind from praying the Eucharist – the best of all prayers – and the sacraments, as they are in a class apart from other prayer.)

The Divine Office (a.k.a. the *Breviary* and / or the *Prayer of the Church*) is not the burden that it was until Vatican II. That Council decreed that in order that the Office be better and more perfectly prayed it was to be 'restored' in accordance with certain principles. The two obvious results of this decree were a) a considerable shortening of the Breviary and b) permission to have it in translation. So nowadays the psalms, prayers and readings of the Divine Office are more accessible. (A Canadian priest once told me how glad he was to have the Breviary in English 'because the only Latin word I know is "Alleluia!".')

There is less excuse nowadays for 'fulfilling the obligation' by merely verbal recitation. It is not too difficult to pay attention to the meaning of at least some of what we are saying. A further advantage is the fact that we should distribute the different parts of the Office throughout the day (where, pre-Vatican II, it was all right to say the whole Office, including Night Prayer, first thing in the morning or, perhaps more commonly, the entire Office, including Morning Prayer, last thing at night).

However, there are suggestions that further reform of the Breviary would help. The 'Office of Readings' (formerly called Matins) could do with a better and wider selection of readings; the Divine Office which diocesan priests are obliged to pray daily is probably still too monastic (i.e. more suited to the needs of a community of monks); and the Breviary should be able to attract wider use by lay people, whether individually or in groups or as the parish community.

The Divine Office is a wonderful treasury (of psalms as Christian prayer, of specifically Christian prayers, and of scripture and other sacred readings) awaiting further discovery and use in the church.

The Rosary is still a favourite prayer for many Catholics, sometimes said in common but more often, I think, by individuals. It used to be said daily by priests and religious, but less so nowadays. Yet Pope John Paul II prayed the Rosary and constantly recommended it to us.

I have found the new 'Mysteries of Light' which Pope John Paul introduced in 2002-2003 to be extremely usable and helpful. Not only do they fill a huge gulf between the Fifth Joyful Mystery and the First Sorrowful Mystery, but they cover the period of Our Lord's public ministry and highlight five events of outstanding importance, each of which challenges us to repeated reflection on its significance.

On a personal note, I am especially glad to have the Transfiguration included as one of the Mysteries of Light. For a number of reasons I have a particular affection for that event and am delighted at its increased prominence in our devotion.

The Transfiguration is relevant for all of us – we need to have our own Tabors in our journey of faith!

Contemplative Prayer is a beautiful experience and, for many, a new discovery. When I was in the seminary, we had a daily period of 'mental prayer' or 'meditation'. We were given some instruction on how to do it and books that provided thoughts for each day's meditation. But I have to admit defeat – probably failure is more accurate. Were the instructions and materials too structured? Or not one's own? Or therefore boring? Or was six o'clock in the morning an unsuitable time?

However, in recent times, there has been the discovery that contemplative prayer is not forbidden territory for ordinary mortals or reserved only for very holy people living in monasteries. The methods are various, the structure much freer, help and advice readily available and, provided we are willing to give the time, the 'technique' is simple and the result a beautiful intimacy with the God who loves us.

Charismatic Prayer has, in the forty or so years since its re-discovery, proved to be a powerful grace for many and a cause of bewilderment, even hostility, for others. Hundreds of books have been written about it but I restrict myself here to some personal reflections.

It is unfortunate, I think, that charismatic renewal became so distinct in the Catholic Church and so differentiated from other ways of praying. Perhaps that was inevitable since charismatic renewal and charismatic prayer take place in groups which meet regularly and therefore are seen as 'different'. Further, these groups were perceived, especially by some who did not join them, as being places of bizarre and even suspect practices (especially 'speaking in tongues') and whose members had an elitist view of themselves.

In reality, charismatic renewal arose from an ardent wish to seek closer union with God, to be more open to the Holy Spirit, to receive the grace of conversion, to be holy (as Vatican II taught). Some gifts of the Holy Spirit which had not been conferred (requested) for centuries were received but so were more usual gifts, maybe with greater intensity (because sought more earnestly).

In a charismatic group there is much use of scripture for prayer and also for learning about God and his plans for us and the world. There should also be authentic teaching by competent persons, prayer of praise, thanksgiving and intercession, and hymns. There can be opportunities for some to witness to God's action in their lives and for people to use God's gifts (which in New Testament Greek are called *charismata* hence 'charismatic').

One of these gifts is called 'speaking in tongues' or, more frequently and simply, 'speaking or singing without words'. If this strikes one as silly or pointless, read what St Augustine said about it early in the fifth century:

This is the way of singing that God gives you: do not search for words. You cannot express in words the sentiments that please God; so praise him with your jubilant singing. This is fine praise of God when you sing with jubilation.

You ask, what is singing in jubilation? It means to realise that words are not enough to express what we are singing in our hearts. At the harvest, in the vineyard, whenever men must labour hard, they begin with songs whose words express their joy. But when their joy brims over and words are not enough, they abandon this coherence and give themselves up to the sheer sound of singing.

What is this jubilation, this exultant song? It is the melody that means our hearts are bursting with feelings that words cannot express. And to whom does this jubilation most belong? Surely to God ... What else can you do when the rejoicing heart has no words and the immensity of your joy will not be imprisoned in speech? What else but 'sing out with jubilation?'

In Scotland Catholic charismatic prayer groups are fewer, smaller and probably less enthusiastic than they were in the 1970s and 1980s. This is at least partly explained, I believe, by the fact that much of what comprises charismatic renewal has al-

ready made its way into mainstream Catholic life in our parishes
– a desire for conversion and holiness, a sense of community,
sharing of faith and prayer, a greater use of scripture and, not
least, the widespread popularity of the contemporary scripture-
based hymns which charismatic prayer groups had known and
used for years.

I first met Catholic charismatic renewal in the summer of
1974 when I was working for a couple of months in St Saviour's
parish in Brooklyn. When subsequently I was parish priest in
Our Lady of Lourdes, East Kilbride, we had a prayer group
which, having had a somewhat embarrassed birth and an extremely fragile infancy, developed into a thriving weekly meeting that brought powerful graces and much happiness to many.

I want to mention one grace of a charismatic prayer group
that sometimes goes unnoticed or unmentioned – the group itself, which gives the participants so much support, friendship
and joy in praying. That was one of the things which I most
missed on leaving the parish – and yet, at the start, I confess that
I had often been glad of an excuse to miss the weekly meetings.

Some final thoughts on prayer. Isn't it good that so many
people want to pray well? And that people see prayer as important and a means to holiness. One indication of this has been the
growth, in Galloway diocese, of weeks of guided prayer. Lay
people, familiar with Ignatian spirituality and trained as prayer
guides, spend a week in any parish community that invites them
to share their knowledge and experience of prayer with individual parishioners seeking guidance and support.

Prayer is more and more on our agenda.

CHAPTER TWENTY

Youth Ministry

When we have meetings to discuss how things are in the parish or in the diocese, you can be fairly sure that someone will ask 'Why is the church not doing more for our youth?'

This always struck me not so much as a question but rather an accusation. The implication (to my guilty mind) seemed to be 'You are the church and you should be doing more for our young people' (and possibly meaning 'our young people who have stopped going to Mass because they say it's boring ').

I count myself fortunate in having had little direct responsibility for parish youth clubs. An early experience (it would be in 1951 or 1952 in Coatbridge) perhaps was sufficiently unnerving that it destroyed any confidence I might have had.

I was told by my parish priest that he thought I should set up a Boys' Guild in the parish. A meeting was called, a reasonable number of teenage boys turned up, and by common consent, indeed acclaim, we decided to form a football team. In those days Boys' Guild teams were frequent in Lanarkshire and there was a league and a cup competition.

Our first venture was to enter the cup tournament and St Bartholomew's, Coatbridge, was drawn against formidable opponents, St Joseph's, Blantyre. We had no kit and very limited funds so I accepted a 'special offer' and bought the necessary jerseys and shorts. The jerseys were light blue in colour and this may have had a psychologically negative effect on our team because we did not do very well.

The referee had no watch so he asked the two touchline 'managers' to let him know when it was time to blow for full-time. I recall, when the score was 16-0 in favour of St Joseph's, saying to my opposite number, 'I think it's time-up', whereupon he looked at his watch and replied, 'No, still two minutes to go.' I am glad to report that, despite their manager's machinations, his team did not add to their score.

I forget what happened to our Boys' Guild but I suspect that our cup experience shattered their morale – and probably has obliterated my recollection of any subsequent activities.

As a teenager myself I had been enrolled in our local parish Boys' Guild. My only memory is of Sunday afternoon meetings in the parochial hall. About twenty of us would turn up and the main item on the agenda was calling the register. This consisted of a member of the Catholic Young Men's Society intoning several hundred names (or so it seemed), the effect being of an interminable succession of names, the great majority followed either by a stony silence or a mumbled suggestion ('not here', 'sick', maybe even 'dead'). An occasional 'present' did little to relieve the total boredom of this weekly performance. Other parishes must have done it better but, at that age, my reactions were limited to an anticipatory dread and a post-meeting sense of relief.

No wonder I feel guilty when someone asks why the church is not doing more for the youth. My heart goes out to fellow inadequates and my total respect to the few, priests or laity, who are blessed with success.

After I became a bishop, people sometimes wrote to me with helpful suggestions. Here is one letter I received, from a young person, with his proposals for a youth-friendly parish:

'I am writing a letter to tell you how I am getting on. I am fine. How are you? The other day at school our teacher told us to write about our ideal parish. My story was like this.

My ideal parish is to have a football team and a club where we could all meet just like a youth club. We could have a disco. We could have one night when all the children could meet and talk about the football games they have played lately and what the telly has been like.' (Ryan, Kilmarnock)

Undoubtedly young people nowadays are generous and thoughtful. They have a highly developed sense of social justice. They will repeatedly help those in need and will protest against instances of institutionalised and social injustice. Issues of justice, peace and the environment are important for them. But older Catholics lament their absence from Mass and their apparent indifference to parish activities and 'churchy' things.

Why, above all, do we see so few teenagers at Mass on Sundays? After all, we say, Mass is not offered as entertainment; it is not what we get out of it but what we put into it.

All of this is true but I do often sympathise with those who say that Mass is boring. Could we not make use of the opportunities and variations available and, without flouting liturgical rules and good taste, be more imaginative?

In addition, there is the menace called peer pressure. Why, to cite the most extreme case, do hundreds of thousands of young people take part so enthusiastically when the Pope holds a World Youth Day? Why do they enjoy Lourdes or Taizé? Such places and events can make us feel very guilty about our own lack of success. One explanation (which I think has much to commend it) is that young people feel comfortable and will be involved provided they know that their peers are present and are also enthusiastic. If others of their generation are not there or are not obvious participants or, worst of all, if they feel that they will be ridiculed for even being there – is it any wonder that they 'vote with their feet'?

I suspect that demanding to know 'What can be done for our youth?' will not solve the problem. I really don't know the answer but I admire the priests and others who try – and the young people who still witness courageously to the faith they have received.

CHAPTER TWENTY-ONE

Pilgrimages

Not everyone enjoys pilgrimages. I suspect they are something of an acquired taste. You know the process: 'No thanks, I don't like being organised', then 'Well I'll go if you think I ought to'; next 'It wasn't as bad as I expected' and finally 'Yes, sure, I'll be there again.'

Of course, we have to admit that pilgrimages nowadays are not nearly as arduous as they once were. Very few people these days can or do spend months in walking great distances to far-off shrines: apart from the danger of being killed or injured by traffic, we are no longer sufficiently fit! But a pilgrimage can still be difficult physically and/or financially.

The essential pilgrimage is the process of getting there rather than having reached one's goal. Even if that be the case, I have to confess that I have visited many shrines but with little effort in getting there – Guadalupe, Esquipulas, Beaupré, Fatima, Santiago de Compostela, Walsingham, Carfin ...

I was a late convert to pilgrimages, both their value and their enjoyment. Perhaps in earlier years I resisted what I imagined would be the organised religiosity of pilgrimages, the enforced communal piety that I thought would be present – or perhaps I was just resistant to community. Whatever it was, I am now pro-pilgrimages and know their importance and the pleasure they can give.

On the last Sunday of August each year the Whithorn pilgrimage takes place, to the town on the south coast of Scotland where St Ninian established the first Christian community in Scotland and to the Cave at the edge of the sea where, two or three miles from the town, the saint would spend periods in solitude and prayer. There is a tradition that, having been converted to Christianity in Rome and entrusted with his mission, he returned to Scotland by way of Tours where he met the great bishop of that city, St Martin. Since the latter died in 397, it has been said that Ninian reached Whithorn the same year. Recent archaeological investigation, however, suggests that the first Christian settlement in Scotland dates, perhaps, from a century later.

Whithorn is a quiet, gentle, little town with its priory church standing amidst the remains and excavations of earlier and famed ecclesiastical shrines and institutions which, for centuries, attracted pilgrims and scholars in great numbers and of all kinds from Scotland and beyond.

On the other side of the wide main street of the town stands the modern Catholic Church of St Martin and St Ninian, built in 1960 to the design of the celebrated London architect, H. S. Goodhart Randel, and commissioned by my predecessor, Bishop Joseph McGee. It is a striking building, in light colours both inside and out, non-traditional in style, which many find attractive and prayerful.

However, the annual pilgrimage continues through the town and on to St Ninian's Cave, the last half mile or so accessible only on foot through Physgill Glen, (a difficult, often muddy track) and along the stony beach (a test for one's feet, legs and balance).

Obviously the weather plays a large role in the annual pilgrimage to Whithorn and, even more, to St Ninian's Cave. There were a few wet and windy occasions in my time but, by God's providence, most pilgrimages took place in beautiful weather or on days on which rain or threatening clouds yielded to sunshine as we arrived for Mass.

Hills enfold the bay, the sea is wide, the outline of the Isle of Man is visible away to the south. The setting is beautiful with the altar placed on a natural platform at the mouth of the Cave and the pilgrims on the beach and on the rocks around, below and even precipitously above. Moreover, despite the difficulty of the terrain, we contrived a fine liturgy with sound system, keyboard or small organ, cantors and full ceremony and involvement, including (perhaps a little boldly but without mishap) communion under both kinds for all. The swampy path and the stony beach were made as easy as possible by hardworking Kilmarnock scouts and guides and the painful walk across the beach seemed shorter by the presence of a faithful pilgrim piper.

The pilgrimage is memorable not only for the natural beauty, but also for the sense of history, tradition and sacred heritage we feel as today's pilgrims worshipping God like so many generations of Christians have done for centuries. It is at such occasions that one has a sense of the faith having been handed down to us and of the presence of God still with his people and making the place sacred.

Of course there are also cheerful aspects to the Whithorn pilgrimage and people do enjoy themselves. I remember the only occasion I was at St Ninian's Cave before I became bishop of the diocese. Bishop McGee invited me to preach at the Mass at the Cave, the day was hot and sunny and, somewhat to my dismay, I noticed, as I began the homily, that a number of the pilgrims had left the Cave to go in for a bathe before returning when the homily was over.

The Galloway custom for many years has been to have our diocesan pilgrimage to Lourdes take place every second year. The routine is too well known to require description but, for me, the great element of a Lourdes pilgrimage is the presence and involvement of the sick. It is they who are central to the pilgrimage. Their spirit, courage and cheerfulness are an inspiration to us all. They are a source of spiritual healing for everyone. For those privileged to be with them – doctors, nurses, helpers (male and female, young and old), priests, everyone – they bring out the best in us. They are the soul of the pilgrimage and the main reason for its success.

Let me make a couple of observations. First, there always seems to be a shortage of nurses and, even more, of helpers, male and female. The work can be long and tiring and does de-

mand sacrifice but it is rewarding in several ways. Indeed I
would go so far as to say that, as a helper, a pilgrim will experience a satisfaction and happiness from the pilgrimage at a
greater intensity than otherwise. Nor can I overstate the value of
the presence of young adults (secondary school age and older).
They are asked to work hard and at unsocial hours but unfailingly it is a good experience for them, and a reassuring witness
to the older pilgrims.

Regrettably it is not cheap to take part in the diocesan pilgrimage to Lourdes. For a week's 'holiday', the price seems ex-
tortionate. Various ways of reducing the cost have been suggested
but without any great success. Perhaps it is a sacrifice that has to
be borne in order to have the graces that a Lourdes pilgrimage
always gives. Miracles in the strict sense of the word are few at
Lourdes, but all of us, sick and healthy, receive true healing
from God, mediated through the Blessed Virgin.

We began Galloway pilgrimages to the Holy Land in the
early 1980s and soon they began to alternate with our Galloway
Lourdes pilgrimages, taking place every second year. Sadly we
have not had any Holy Land pilgrimages since September 2000
due to the increased violence.

For me the Holy Land pilgrimage (I have been there about
twelve times) is always a wonderful experience. The reasons are
obvious – the opportunity to be in the land where Jesus lived, to
see the hills and valleys, the plains and the mountains which he
knew, to sail on the Sea of Galilee on which he sailed (and
walked), to visit the churches and shrines which mark the great
events of his life in Bethlehem. Nazareth, Capernaum and
Jerusalem. And to be on pilgrimage with other people of faith, to
share their happiness, to witness the awed delight of first-timers
– all of these greatly enhance the experience of being a pilgrim in
the Holy Land.

I have a particular affection for Mount Tabor. It is a high hill
standing in splendid isolation in southern Galilee. No doubt
Jesus, Peter, James and John climbed it the hard way, whereas
today's pilgrims are conveyed in taxis, up a road with over

twenty hairpin bends and with drivers who take perverse pleasure in making the pilgrims fear for their very lives. The cool air,
the breeze and the magnificent views from the summit are part
of the pleasure of being there but it is the sense of peace, the
tranquillity, the atmosphere that refreshes the soul and reas-
sures the pilgrim which I most associate with Tabor. It is something I often recall, aware that, like Jesus and the apostles on
their way to the events that awaited them in Jerusalem, we also,
on our life pilgrimage, need our Tabors, our experience of God's
reassurance for our future.

Of course one cannot be a pilgrim in the Holy Land without
being aware of the people who live there and of the sadness of
their lives. There is still violence and conflict, innocent people
are being killed or maimed and, generally, people live in fear
and with little hope of peace. It is a dreadful situation and so
pitifully ironic that all this should be happening in the land
called holy. The violence is to be condemned but that is not sufficient. One has to ask why there is such violence, what causes it.
The reason is injustice and I believe that the world must not only
condemn the violence but also be courageous enough to name
the injustices and do all it can to put an end to them. Much easier
said than done but I think that the violence will not be ended by
'defeating the terrorists' until we have also ended the injustices
that produce them. May God help the Holy Land, its Christians
(who, sadly, are emigrating in large numbers to seek a peaceful
life) and all its inhabitants, Jewish and Moslem as well as
Christian.

My first visit to the Holy Land was in 1963 when Jerusalem
was still a divided city, (the newer western part being in Israel,
the Old City in Jordan). We landed at Ramallah airport from
Beirut and, some days later, crossed from Arab to Jewish
Jerusalem through the Mandelbaum Gate (the only crossing
point) and a walk of 100 metres or so in No Man's Land from an
Arab taxi to a Jewish one. We needed two passports since an
Israeli stamp on a passport meant denial of entry to any Arab
country. After only one day and a night in Israeli Jerusalem we

were advised to leave because quite near where we were staying firing broke out between Israeli and Jordanian troops. Hearing the gunfire was alarming and many thought that it could escalate into a prolonged and more widespread engagement.

My later visits were subsequent to the Six Days War in 1967 so all the city of Jerusalem (as well as other Holy Land territory) had been incorporated into Israel and, though tension remained and was sometimes palpable, I did not experience any further violence.

I have said that I really enjoy pilgrimages, not only because of the locations and their associations but also because the company of so many 'brothers and sisters in Christ' is always, for me, an enriching experience.

There is another reason also. The image of the church that I find the most helpful is that of the pilgrim church. A pilgrimage is the church in miniature, a living illustration of what the church should be and is – a band of people with a common purpose and goal, travelling thither together, but inevitably with stragglers and strugglers, even some getting lost now and again; not too regimented as if on a route march but keeping our own individuality, ready to support, help, forgive and enjoy one another, and animated by a faith that allows us to be aware of the presence of Christ in our midst, encouraging us to continue in faith and hope and without fear.

Yes, there is nothing like a pilgrimage to enable us to know who and what we are in God's sight.

CHAPTER TWENTY-TWO

Politics

'The church should keep out of politics.' Yes, I agree that those who 'speak for the church' should not use that privilege in order to support or promote one side of a political issue or dispute – provided the issue is not one that involves morality as well as politics. In other words, many political issues are also ethical issues and, in such cases, the church has the right, indeed the duty, of making its teaching known. This duty is not to be restricted to matters of individual morality.

There are obvious examples of political issues which are also moral issues, such as a country's legislation on abortion and euthanasia but, in today's climate, the moral or ethical dimension of many problems is ignored or not understood and, as a result, there is a resentment at what is seen as church 'interference'. But to keep quiet to avoid offence or resentment would be a dereliction of duty. As well as the right to life, I am thinking also of issues of social justice and human rights, of relations between the affluent nations and the 'developing' world.

There is one issue current in this country that may, or may not, have its ethical dimension, so when I give my own opinion I am speaking only personally and as a citizen and not in any way presuming to 'speak for the church'.

I refer to the controversy regarding Britain and Europe. Should we approve the European Constitution? Should we change our currency to the euro? Should we leave, or stay in, the European Union?

I am a European and pro-European. I want to share in the culture of our continent as fully as possible, to be a citizen of a country with full membership in the community of Europe.

Moreover I believe that the EU (in its earlier and developing stages, as it is now and as it will grow in the future) is our best safeguard for peace in a continent riven by conflict and violence since history began; as well as a means of bringing friendship, acceptance, toleration and co-operation to the nations and peoples whom it comprises.

The arguments against seem to me to be weak. At their worst, I suspect there is at times an element of xenophobia (and maybe even of religious antipathy) which is non-Christian and perhaps, to some extent at least, based on ignorance and fear.

Also weak, in my opinion, are the arguments (both pro and con, actually) that put all their emphasis on whether 'it will be good for us'. 'Will it be to Britain's advantage?' seems to me to be a very selfish criterion if it does not also take into account the benefits to others of our being in (or not in). 'National interest' may seem an obvious yardstick – but is it not also a selfish one? Indeed, if our country possesses so many advantages should we not be sharing them rather than keeping them to ourselves?

Words can be demonised so that sometimes it is necessary only to mention them in order to dismiss what they signify as unacceptable – such words as constitution, integration, community, federation. Moreover, arguments against Europe often presume, erroneously, that Britain has been one nation for a thousand years or more – 'our parliament', 'our legal system', 'our currency'. Have they never heard what happened in 1707 or that, even today, not all of Britain has the same legal and education systems as England? There is an arrogance, I hope unconscious, in such specious assumptions.

My pro-European views are, I suspect, in part the result of my having lived 'on the continent' for fifteen years, six in Italy and nine in Spain. I feel at home in Europe, I like the people, the music, the art, the scenery and the food. Even if Britain were to leave the EU, I could still go abroad and enjoy those things – but I do hope that we shall grasp the chance of becoming genuinely citizens of Europe as well as of our own nation.

Let us not stand aside, an island race that wants little part in

European civilisation and culture, content to see 'the continent' as not much more than a trading partner or a holiday destination.

It is encouraging to know that the Holy See and the Council of European Bishops' Conferences (CCEE) are strong and constant supporters of European integration. But perhaps that very support which they give is part of the problem for Britain.

CHAPTER TWENTY-THREE

Music

When I was ten years old, all the children in our class were graded for singing – A,B or C. I was put among the Cs.

Then when I was in my first year in the seminary (I was 16 or 17), we each got a turn of singing the solo which opened Compline in Latin: *Iube Domine, benedicere ... Noctem quietam et finem perfectum ...* The prospect of making a fool of myself made me almost sick with fear, but the reality was even worse than I dreaded. It was one of those occasions when I should have been happy for the ground to open and swallow me.

Despite those incidents (which I remember vividly and with embarrassment), I love music and enjoy singing (as long as I am one among several).

I trace my awakening to the delights of music to a quartet of musicians who, again when I was 16 or 17, were brought to Blairs College one evening to entertain us young seminarians. Their programme was a series of popular classics which were totally new to me. Until then I had imagined classical music to be highbrow and boring. The quartet played Delibes' *Pizzicato Polka*, some of Saint Saens' *Carnival of the Animals*, Sibelius' *Valse Triste*, and a few other pieces. I thoroughly enjoyed that concert when 'good music' was revealed to me.

When I was in the army, I saw my first opera – Puccini's *La Bohème* – and enjoyed it even if my sixpence (or shilling) got me only a standing place in the gods of a Belfast theatre. As students in Rome we frequently went to the Sunday evening concerts in the Teatro Argentina. The orchestra was usually the Accademia di Santa Cecilia but there were famous guest conductors and soloists – and on one occasion, a concert with Beniamino Gigli.

He was the second world famous tenor I had heard. When I was much younger, my father took me to a church hall to hear Sir Harry Lauder, then semi-retired. 'You will be able to say that you once saw and heard the great Harry Lauder', my father impressed on me.

Over the years my tastes have become wider – not just symphonies and operas, but chamber music of many kinds – and especially of course the great Spanish composers: Falla, Granados, Albéniz, Rodrigo … But I have to confess a difficulty in appreciating and enjoying what I suppose may be called contemporary music. Enough of this, however, because what I really meant to write about is church music and music in the liturgy.

Before I went to Blairs College in 1942, my experience of church music was limited to a small number of hymns that comprised the choir's repertoire in my home parish: *I rise from dreams of time, Sweet Sacrament divine, I'll sing a hymn to Mary* and a few others.

The seminary introduced me to singing plain chant at Sunday High Mass. We had to learn and sing the various settings of the Common of the Mass (*Missa de Angelis, Credo III* etc). In addition, each week we practised the Proper of the Mass for the following Sunday : introit, gradual, offertory and communion antiphons. For this each of us had acquired a thick volume called the *Liber Usualis*. For some months I was bewildered – I would vaguely follow the notes which accompanied the text of the introit but was totally mystified how we got through in such a short time the much greater number of notes which accompanied the text of the gradual. The mystery was eventually solved for me. Apparently we were simply using a psalm tone for the gradual (and not the full version) but that had not been explained (or if it was, I missed it).

I never cared much for the plain chant of the Mass, especially the Propers. Had we had a monastic choir properly trained, it would probably have been more attractive to me – but I particularly disliked choir practice and must have been a trial for successive choir masters.

Since English began to be used in the liturgy, church music has, of course, changed greatly. Much of it I find inspiring, moving and enjoyable – not only hymns but also settings of the liturgical texts and especially of the Mass. When the diocese of Galloway was preparing to celebrate 1997, the sixteenth centenary of its foundation by St Ninian, I asked James MacMillan, an Ayrshire man brought up in Cumnock, to compose a Mass setting. The result was *The Galloway Mass*, for which he refused to accept any fee and with which he honoured me by dedicating it to me.

As bishop I tried to encourage singing at Mass – not only suitable and good hymns but also, and more importantly, the parts of the Mass themselves. Some parts make little sense if not sung (the Acclamations) but it is also better if the psalm is sung. Many parishes responded very courageously and successfully – but I sometimes feel a) that, when the psalm is sung and there are four or five verses, it can be disproportionately long, especially if the first reading is a short one, and b) that, when a parish does not have a cantor to sing the psalm verses, a psalm-based hymn could be sung by the congregation, instead of merely 'saying' the psalm.

I do not like paraphrases of, for example, the Gloria or the Sanctus, especially if the same melody is used for all the sung parts (which have very different themes and moods, from joyful praise to a prayer for forgiveness). And to return to the psalm, it should bear some relation to the foregoing reading.

People sometimes say that they would prefer 'a quiet Mass, with no singing' but I feel that such a request is a little unreasonable since some Mass texts should be sung, and not to sing them diminishes that liturgy.

The subject of music in church is, of course, a difficult one and can produce very mixed reactions and bad feelings. But most of us, I believe, are grateful for the fact that our worship, and especially at Mass, allows us to participate more fully by the fact that it contains music – and not just for a choir but for everyone to sing. Though well-known, St Augustine's point is worth recalling: 'They who sing pray twice.'

PART FOUR

Central America

CHAPTER TWENTY-FOUR

Central America: First Impressions

One of the most enriching and interesting aspects of my life has been my association with Central America. It all began in 1984 when I attended a meeting in Glasgow, organised by SCIAF and at which the Catholic Institute for International Relations (CIIR) had been invited to speak of its work in Central America. CIIR had been founded as 'Sword of the Spirit' during World War II and its work is described as 'tackling the causes of poverty and injustice internationally through advocacy and skill sharing'. It is active in countries in Asia, Africa, and Latin America and, in addition, seeks to raise awareness at home of issues of poverty and injustice in the developing world.

At that meeting in Glasgow, the principal speaker was Fr Ricardo Falla, a Jesuit anthropologist who was living and working with Guatemalan 'internal refugees', indigenous Mayan people in hiding from the Guatemalan army which was pursuing a policy of near genocide against them. Fr Falla was accompanied that day by the then head of the Latin American desk of CIIR, Mrs Kathy Piper. She told me that CIIR (which is based in London) wanted to have more visibility in Scotland. To that end, would I (as bishop and able to speak Spanish) consider being made a vice-president of the Institute? I readily agreed – and thus began a series of visits to Central America that taught me so much about those lands and their peoples – friendly, welcoming, beautiful yet, in so many cases, impoverished, oppressed and persecuted.

My first visit to Central America took place in October/ November 1984. We were a party of four: Kathy Piper, Bishop James O'Brien (auxiliary in Westminster), Duncan MacLaren (executive director, Scottish Catholic International Aid Fund) and myself. That first visit I found fascinating, disturbing and very bewildering.

We spent a day in Mexico City where we met a number of exiled Guatemalan church people. Kathy Piper knew the issues being discussed – but I had little idea of what was being spoken about; moreover, I found it difficult to understand what people were saying. But Bishop O'Brien and I did manage a quick visit to the Basilica of Nuestra Señora de Guadalupe!

Guatemala City seemed unattractive to me – narrow, crowded, dirty streets, a somewhat menacing atmosphere (we knew that the regime was cruel and tyrannical and used death squads as well as informers) but the Hotel del Centro was clean and comfortable, with a bar, restaurant, a pianist and a singer. During our days in the capital we had many meetings with priests, religious, human rights groups, women whose husbands had been murdered or abducted; but, on that first visit, I am afraid that I didn't really get fully in touch – due partly to my ignorance of the specific matters under discussion, partly to my (then) poor comprehension skills.

On the Sunday morning we went to the outskirts of the city for an open-air Mass. The priest was a Belgian missionary who told us that, in the congregation, there were '*orejas*' (ears, i.e. informers ready to carry tales to the authorities about what he said). The number of small evangelical churches was also evident. Many of them are financed by US evangelicals, they are hostile to the Catholic Church – but many Catholics have joined them and they are much more acceptable to the authorities than is the Catholic Church.

During my stay in Guatemala, the group made one excursion outside the capital – to the province of Quiché in the northwest highlands. Quiché has a majority of indigenous inhabitants and it is probably the area that has suffered most from the activities of the Guatemalan army. Many thousands of people (including many catechists and other active Catholics) have been brutally killed or 'disappeared', the people there have endured a reign of terror, the inhumanity and savagery of which can scarcely be exaggerated. On that first occasion, in Quiché, we visited only two centres, both in the south of the province: Santa Cruz, the provincial capital where we met the apostolic administrator, Mons Urízar (there being no bishop at the time), and Chichicastenango, where we lodged in the beautiful (but almost empty) Hotel Santo Tomás (a former monastery) and marvelled at the exotic market which sold anything and everything but especially the wonderful woven cloth in such a variety of bright colours and so typical of Guatemala. The huge church of Santo Tomás was packed for the feast of All Saints. It was a brilliant liturgy with clouds of incense and enthusiastic singing accompanied by 'conjuntos' of accordions and marimbas. Duncan MacLaren had written out for me, and coached me how to say, a phrase of greeting in Quiché language. I delivered it nervously and it was received in total silence (possibly out of respect for a visiting bishop but much more probably because my pronunciation was awful and totally unintelligible).

From Guatemala we continued to Nicaragua. The differences were immediately obvious. The country had had its revolution, the tyrannical and murderous Somoza regime was gone, the left-wing Sandinistas were in power, the people, though living in great poverty, were not living in fear and terror. There were no distinctive indigenous people – all were of European descent or mixed race (with people of African descent on the Atlantic coast).

We were given lodgings in the house of the Jesuit Fathers who taught in the University of Central America. (The university rector, Fr César Jerez SJ, gave me his room.) I soon learned that the university, its faculty and many other priests were viewed with hostility and suspicion by the Archbishop of Managua, Cardinal Obando y Bravo SDB, and most of the bishops for their support of the revolution and the new Sandinista government.

During that first visit, we had meetings with several of the Jesuits, with religious and with a number of government people (all of whom seemed intelligent, very aware of the problems which the country faced, yet determined to do all they could to bring health, education and a better future to the people of Nicaragua). Once again, however, as in Guatemala, I felt frustrated that, because I was unfamiliar with the issues discussed and slow to pick up what people were saying, I did not contribute to the discussions as I should have liked.

One obvious element in the situation both in Guatemala and Nicaragua was the role of the United States. Menacing, bullying, interfering and with a very right-wing agenda (that tended to equate anything else as Marxist and therefore unacceptable), the United States was implicated in the Guatemalan army's strategy of terror against the indigenous population; while it was promoting and equipping the armed resistance of the so-called 'Contras' against the government and the great majority of the people of Nicaragua.

Although it was my first experience of Central America and I was not nearly as aware of the situation as I later became, I was interviewed, on my return to Scotland, by Brian Wilson (later MP for North Ayrshire) and his report appeared in *New Statesman* for 23 November 1984.

Bishop Maurice Taylor of Galloway says ... the Guatemalan bishops – on the basis of what they understand Lord Colville's findings to be – are 'distraught that a man of such experience and influence could put in such a report'.

Lord Colville of Culross ... was until last year British representative on the United Nations Human Rights Commission. ... He was appointed to carry out a special report on Guatemala and completed his researches in September.

Bishop Taylor asserts 'Wherever we went, people were complaining about this very unsatisfactory report put in by Lord Colville, a UN appointed observer who couldn't speak Spanish and who went around with representatives of the Guatemalan government.'

Bishop Taylor was deeply impressed to meet a group of representatives from the wives, mothers and sisters of 225 men who have disappeared in recent months. 'We hope that by speaking out we'll be doing something for the people of Guatemala. We were so convinced of the evils of the regime and the violations of human rights as well as the restrictions on the practice of religion.

Of the current regime, (Bishop Taylor says) 'There's no sign that the army of Guatemala intends to relinquish its total control of power or to implement serious reforms – such as the desperately needed agrarian reform. Without such fundamental structural changes, there appears no hope that the situation of gross injustice and fear will come to an end in the near future.'

In response to Bishop Taylor, Lord Colville emphasises that his report hasn't yet been published and says he assumes that any conjecture about what it will say must be based on a press conference he gave in Guatemala.

'It's a document intended to be read as a whole,' he says. 'Some things I am critical of, some things I give them a pat on the back for. The bishop will have to wait and see what's in the report.' Lord Colville isn't prepared to go into it in more detail pre-publication.

Lord Colville responds to the criticism of his appropriateness on linguistic grounds by saying that he can speak Spanish, but not speak it very well. 'There isn't time for me to fumble around with a language at which I am not very good.'

CHAPTER TWENTY-FIVE

El Salvador

El Salvador is by far the smallest of the Central American republics (the books all say it is approximately the size of Wales) and it is the only one lacking two coastlines – it has only a Pacific coast. Its people are possibly the most energetic and combative in Central America and their history is at least as violent as any in the region.

The recent civil war began in 1980 in a country where military dictatorship and right wing tyranny were the rule. There was an oligarchy of fourteen powerful families who owned most of the land and most of the wealth. Death squads (murderers hired by the army and their associates) were very active; tens of thousands of people were killed in the violence of the 1970s and 1980s. It was perhaps inevitable that a popular uprising should take place, which it did in 1980 with the creation of a guerilla army, the FMLN (the *Farabundo Martí* National Liberation Front). The civil war continued into the 1990s, there were thousands of casualties, the death squads were active, people lived in terror – the whole country was in a state of confusion. Since the ceasefire, the FMLN (or its political successor) has gained many successes in local elections but has not yet defeated ARENA, the conservative right-wing party favoured by El Salvador's rich and powerful (a party formed by Roberto D'Aubuisson, who, in all probability, was guilty of many crimes, especially murders carried out by death squads).

Although the country is officially at peace, the post-war years have brought a lot of violence – kidnapping, armed robbery, revenge killing – due, probably, to the number of guns and ex-combatants available, as well as to drug-trafficking, and to widespread poverty.

I visited El Salvador many times since 1984 – and continue to do so. On a CIIR delegation in 1990, I was asked by a priest of the archdiocese of St Andrews and Edinburgh, who was then working as a parish priest of the diocese of Chalatenango in the northern war zone of El Salvador, if I could find a priest to supply for him while he took some leave in Britain. The possibility seemed very attractive to me personally so I decided to give myself a ten or twelve week sabbatical and undertake to do the supply myself. Since canon law states that a bishop should not be away from his diocese for more than a month each year, I wrote to Rome for permission. After a long delay, a reply came back – my request was most unusual, it said but, for this one occasion, permission was granted. My account of those few months in the parish of Dulce Nombre de María is to be found in *El Salvador: Portrait of a Parish*.

Of course most of the events which made news all over the world took place in the capital, San Salvador. One such event was the murder of the city's archbishop, Oscar Romero. When made archbishop he was not expected to 'rock the boat' but, in fact, the almost daily violence changed him and he became increasingly courageous in his condemnation of the assassinations and the atrocities either carried out or tolerated by the army and the government. His weekly homilies, broadcast throughout the nation, were particularly outspoken and he began to receive ominous threats. Finally on Monday 24 March 1980 he was shot by a hired marksman (who may himself then have been shot by his hirers as a 'precaution') as he celebrated Mass in the convent chapel of the Hospitalito de la Divina Providencia (a little hospital run by religious sisters and where the archbishop lived very simply in a cottage in the grounds).

Archbishop Romero's body is in a tomb in the crypt of San Salvador cathedral and, despite Rome's reluctance (or at least slowness) in proceeding towards canonisation, he is popularly venerated as a saint by most Salvadoreans. One can visit the chapel where he was killed and the cottage (which I have done more than once).

I have been fortunate enough to have met Archbishop Arturo Rivera y Damas (Romero's successor and also a heroic figure who unfortunately died very suddenly) and the present archbishop, Fernando Sainz Lacalle (Spanish and a member of Opus Dei) as well as the auxiliary bishop , Gregorio Rosa Chávez (who was one of Archbishop Romero's closest collaborators).

Nowadays there is not the same degree of tension between the archdiocese and the civil authorities, in large measure due to the great decrease in government and army violence against citizens, especially articulate and socially concerned Catholics.

It is astonishing that, at the funeral Mass for Archbishop Romero, only one of the bishops from other dioceses in El Salvador was present (most of them disagreed with Romero's outspoken criticisms of the regime) but many foreign bishops were there. As the crowds left the cathedral at the end of the Mass, shots were fired at them from the windows of the National Palace and several people were killed.

Another event in San Salvador which made the country's reputation even grimmer took place on 16 November 1989 – the assassination of six Jesuit priests, faculty members of the University of Central America, along with their housekeeper and her teenage daughter. UCA had been for some years critical of the human rights record of the Salvadorean government and army and one night, during a period of great tension and fear in the city, a death squad (commissioned and protected by the authorities) entered the Jesuits' residence, ordered the six priests to go to the little garden outside and shot them there in cold blood. Because of the tension, the two women had been advised not to walk home after work that day but, for safety's sake, to spend the night in the residence. To prevent their being able to give their account of the priests' murders, they also were taken out and shot.

A few months before the crime, our CIIR delegation had visited the university and had been welcomed and shown round by Fr Segundo Montes SJ, soon to be one of the victims. On later visits to the country, I have tried to make a little pilgrimage to the university and the place where the Jesuits and the two women were murdered. Their residence has been refurbished and is again in use. There is a small museum which tells the story of the murder and has various documents, photographs and personal articles on view and, perhaps most moving, the little garden has now six red rose bushes and two white, planted and blooming on the spot where the bodies were found after the crime. The tombs of the six priests are on one side of the sanctuary in the modern university chapel – now very much a shrine to their memory – only a few steps from their residence. May they rest in peace.

I met some remarkable people in El Salvador – people who have suffered greatly, people with dreadful memories, heroic people. Among these last, I must mention María Julia Hernández, director of *Tutela Legal* ('Legal Protection'), the human rights office of the archdiocese of San Salvador. *Tutela Legal* was formed in 1982 and María Julia has been its director from the start. She is a small, affable, friendly person who sits behind a desk totally covered with documents, reports, letters and other papers to a height of at least a foot – but she is a remarkably active lady, always ready to travel to anywhere in the country where she is needed.

The work that she and her staff do is to monitor the human rights situation, to investigate reports of murders and disappearances, to follow up people's complaints of torture or ill-treatment in prisons (especially pre-trial treatment etc.). When I visited her in 2004, she told me that she has to work as hard as ever, investigating war crimes, clandestine cemeteries which have been discovered, complaints by victims of injustices. El Salvador, she said, had more violent deaths in 2003 than had occurred in the final years of the civil war.

The following morning she was leaving at 3am to drive to a distant town to investigate certain allegations about human rights violations. She is indefatigable, fearless (she could have been murdered or 'disappeared' on many occasions when her reports were unwelcome to the authorities), truly heroic.

It is through knowing people like María Julia Hernández that one is humbled and yet enriched, aware that Central America, though it has suffered so much from poverty, violence and injustice, can also be so uplifting to one's spirit and make one praise God for such goodness and beauty.

CHAPTER TWENTY-SIX

Nicaragua

Nicaragua is, in many ways, a bizarre country, certainly different from its Central American neighbours and even, it seems to me, surreal. It endured the cruel tyranny of the Somoza dynasty from 1937 until the revolution in 1979 led by the Sandinistas – FSLN (*Frente Sandinista Liberación Nacional* – named after Augusto César Sandino who led an unsuccessful revolt in 1920 and was later executed).

Elections held in 1980 and again in 1984 returned the Sandinistas under the presidency of their leader, Daniel Ortega. While in power, they distributed the vast lands of the Somoza family and began successful national health and literacy campaigns.

Since 1981, guerilla warfare led by the 'Contras' against the Sandinistas had been a serious problem, especially since the Contras were supported financially, politically and militarily by the United States which did everything it could to destabilise the country.

A peace agreement was reached in 1988 and, in the subsequent general elections, the Sandinistas were unexpectedly defeated. Since then Nicaragua has been ruled by right-wing governments (some of whose leaders are now in jail for fraud and corruption) and the Sandinistas have been weakened by internal splits and have so far failed to regain power.

I visited Nicaragua several times during the 1980s from 1984 onwards. Let me quote from the report made by our CIIR delegation of 1987:

'Managua must be one of the strangest of all capital cities. The centre was almost totally flattened in the 1972 earthquake and, because of the continuing danger and the need to use available funds for other purposes, it has not been re-built. To stand and look around gives one the eerie impression of being somewhere that is a cross between Pompeii and Hiroshima. The cathedral is roofless and overgrown with weeds, the National Palace (the former parliament building) has been patched up and is in use as government offices, the Intercontinental Hotel stands in splendid isolation and the rebuilt National Stadium was solemnly inaugurated during our visit. (Ironically the occasion was marked by an international baseball series – the Nicaraguans may be at odds with the US, but they love the US national game – with teams from Nicaragua, Cuba, Mexico and the Dominican Republic). But there is little else except the streets, neatly and regularly intersecting a vast area of grassland.

As a result, 'sprawling' is a word that might have been coined with Managua in mind, since a large number of widely separated suburbs have been constructed. Even if you have transport, it is extremely difficult to locate an address and, of course, for the great majority of people who are without cars and who must rely on the skeletal bus service, the daily journey from home to work and back is an ordeal.' (CIIR/SCIAF, *A Thousand Times Heroic*, 1988, p 64)

It was obvious that the Catholic Church in Nicaragua was divided in its attitude to the Sandinistas. The bishops, some priests and some lay people were against them and regarded the government as Marxist and dangerous. On the other hand, most religious (male and female), many diocesan priests and most lay people supported the Sandinistas. It was an unhappy division and produced a lot of bitterness.

During our visits to Nicaragua, we had many meetings with government ministers and officials and with religious leaders. Perhaps the two most interesting occasions were our meetings with Cardinal Miguel Obando y Bravo SDB and with Violeta Chamorro.

Despite many requests the archbishop of Nicaragua was unable to see us until at last he agreed to a short meeting early one morning. He was courteous but very firm in his dislike of the Sandinista government. This attitude made him very unpopular with many Nicaraguans ('the church once again siding with the rich') but he did not seem upset by this. He had, of course, the support of the Vatican for his stance (exemplified by his being made a cardinal in 1985 and, for many years, the only Central American member of the Sacred College).

The Chamorro family is famous in Nicaragua. Violeta's husband was murdered by the Somocistas and her children were to be found in the ranks of the Sandinistas and the Contras. She herself (at the time we met her she was owner and editor of a daily newspaper but she later became the country's president) was violently against the Sandinistas, fanatically so and to such an extent that I thought she was unbalanced. The meeting was a strange experience. She talked incessantly and her views were totally black and white. It must have been one of her bad days. I believe that, when she became president, her manner, if not her politics, was more controlled.

(I did not meet Daniel Ortega in Nicaragua but did so later, when he was given a civic reception in Glasgow and attended Sunday Mass in St Aloysius' Church in the city. I remember that, at the reception, he pointed to Cardinal Winning and asked me if he was a Catholic.)

Several times during CIIR delegations to Nicaragua, we left the capital to visit other parts of the country. One such visit, in 1987, is especially noteworthy and I quote the account of it which we included in our subsequent published report.

The most memorable experience we had in Nicaragua was the weekend we spent with Father John Medcalf of Arundel and Brighton diocese, the only English priest working in Nicaragua. Father Medcalf is parish priest in an area of the Atlantic Coast region, deep in the war zone.

Two weeks before we arrived the parish had been the target of a Contra attack, along with four other towns along the Rama road, the only road that connects the Atlantic Coast region with Managua.

In his regular newsletter Father Medcalf described what happened:

'On October 15 this village of Muelle was attacked by over 500 well-equipped Contras. The battle began at 3 a.m. and continued uninterrupted until 6 a.m. The din of mortars, machine-guns and ricocheting shrapnel was horrendous. The attackers penetrated simultaneously at three different points – the high road, the bridge over Monkey River and Death Canyon. Their chief objective was probably to blow up the bridge.

The Contras surged into several of the village streets. We heard them shouting slogans. The Sandinistas made a temporary retreat, only to return with reinforcements for the street fighting. The bridge was saved and the Contras dispersed when their supply of ammunition came to an end.

We opened up the parish hall to the wounded and dead. They were brought in from all parts of the village. Our canvas stretcher-beds were quickly drenched in blood since we used them for those worst wounded. Others were laid on the tiled floor. I have so many indelible impressions of that day ... There were more than 30 gravely injured and 20 dead. The morning seemed endless as we waited for an ambulance to transport the injured to hospital.

Rumours began to reach us that four other villages had been attacked that night. At 2 p.m. a Sandinista driver made a bad mistake. Having found the dead bodies of three Contras near the bridge, he strung them up on the back of his open lorry, heads down, like sides of beef bound for an unhygienic market. The driver's fury was understandable, but many villagers protested as he drove through the streets with the almost naked bodies waving grotesquely. I spoke with the mayor and we agreed to give them a Christian burial in a common grave in the village cemetery, as soon as possible. There were no more coffins available by this hour of the day, but by 4 p.m. the three soldiers had been buried in plastic sheeting and a rustic cross marks their grave.'

When we arrived in Muelle de los Bueyes, where the

parish house and centre are located, the people were still stunned by the attack. There was a constant, pervasive fear that there could be a repeat attack and for that weekend we experienced what it is like to live with that kind of insecurity and tension, never knowing when the Contras will strike again and listening all night to the exchange of fire as the fighting raged a few miles away.

There was also the moment, about 11 p.m., of sheer and sudden terror when a machine-gun opened up right outside the presbytery and convent where we were staying. We immediately jumped – literally! – to the conclusion that the Contras had invaded the village again and that we were caught in the middle of a battle. In fact, the cause of the disturbance was one of the villagers who regularly got drunk and liked to mark the occasion by firing off a few bursts. Some of the party were given this explanation immediately, others not until the next morning. For the latter it was a long and anxious night.

Our journey from Managua to Muelle had not been without incident … Until we reached Juigalpa we had seen very few people on the road and little sign of any special security measures. On the second stage of the journey, however, it was very different – we were now in 'Contra territory'. Bridges over every stream and gully – and there are many in this rolling hill country – are guarded by the military and a good many carry signs indicating that the area around the bridge has been mined. At one point we had to make a slight detour when we reached one bridge which had been badly damaged in the Contra attack on the night described by Father Medcalf.

From time to time we came across open trucks packed with people jammed shoulder to shoulder in the back – Nicaragua's inter-city express coach service. The journey to Muelle de los Bueyes taught us many things about the daily hardships and difficulties faced by many ordinary people in Nicaragua.

There are approximately 40,000 people in Father John's parish, which is made up of several small towns or villages and 66 outlying hamlets. The parish centre is located in

Muelle de los Bueyes, where we stayed. The parish has a team of two priests, three Franciscan sisters from the United States and six deacons. There are also 120 delegates of the Word and 500 catechists. The sisters' home had been caught in the crossfire during the recent battle and was now, as they commented, 'air-conditioned' by bullet holes. As in other parts of Central America, the area covered by the parish is huge and the priests can get to the various hamlets only once every few months when they go out on one of their regular 'safaris'. The journeys are very arduous and involve long distances which have to be covered on foot, on horseback or by mule through difficult jungle terrain.

There is also always a danger of running into groups of armed Contras, as indeed both priests have done in the past. Sunday Mass is a rarity in the remote areas and the weekly religious celebration is usually led by a delegate who conducts a Liturgy of the Word and presides at the distribution of Communion. The delegates of the Word, here as elsewhere in the region, are of any age and either sex, but are chosen not only for leadership qualities but also because of their exemplary lives. Another quality required in delegates is courage. In other parts of Central America they are often seen as a threat to privilege and wealth, and become victims of the army's suspicion and repressive measures; some have been killed, others tortured, kidnapped or imprisoned. In this part of Nicaragua the delegates face similar dangers, but in this case it is from the Contras, who have often targeted delegates of the Word, along with health workers and teachers, as being supporters of the Sandinistas.

On Sunday morning we went with Father Medcalf along the Rama road and across the bridge which had been the Contras' target in the recent attack, to the nearby village of Cara de Mono (literally 'Monkey Face' but, in deference to the feelings of its inhabitants, also called Santa Ana, which is the name of the parish church), where we joined the local community for Mass. It was a most moving experience, especially when some mothers in the congregation, who had lost sons in the war, began to speak of their pain and sadness. It was the day before All Souls' Day (the Day of the Dead), a very important day in Latin America. The delegate of the Word in this village is also the local midwife and a (very fit and active) grandmother. She told us that she has to carry a gun when she is carrying out her duties because health workers are a particular target of the Contras. It is a sad irony that this woman, whose job it is to assist in bringing new life into the world, is forced to carry an instrument of death.

The following day we returned to Managua but, before leaving Muelle, we celebrated Mass. It was All Souls' Day and Mass with the people of Muelle, several of whom had sons killed, was a poignant and memorable occasion. We were privileged to share in their grief and in their faith. Our last act, as we drove out of the village, was to stop at the cemetery (thronged that day) and to pray at the graves of the young men, both Sandinistas and Contras, who had lost their lives in such a tragic and needless way. (CIIR/SCIAF, *A Thousand Times Heroic*, 1988, pp 64-68)

Through all their woes, the Nicaraguans have not lost their mordant wit. 'Poor Nicaragua', they would say, 'God seems to send us one disaster after another – the Somoza dictatorship, the 1972 earthquake, hurricanes, the papal visit ...' This referred to Pope John Paul's pastoral visit in 1983 when, at the open-air Mass in Managua, some mothers pleaded with the Pope to pray for their sons killed by the Contras. The Holy Father became very angry and ordered them to be silent – a most embarrassing incident which, along with the Pope's public rebuke to those priests who were ministers in the Sandinista government, left Nicaraguans with unpleasant memories of the papal visit to their country.

Since then, Nicaragua's troubles have continued – a rolling back of the literacy and health campaigns set up by the Sandinista government, a devastating hurricane in 1998, a severe drought in 2001 – and most of the population still living at subsistence level or worse.

CHAPTER TWENTY-SEVEN

Honduras and Costa Rica

Having been in Honduras on only two occasions (both times as a member of CIIR delegations), my experience of the country is very limited and my impressions superficial.

Honduras is a country in which the civilian population is tightly controlled by the military, where most of the people live in poverty and which, compared to other Central American republics, has shown little organised resistance to a repressive regime. To an extent this may be due to some limited land reform in the 1970s but traditionally the Hondurans see themselves as lacking the energy, initiative or drive that would produce violent and armed resistance. 'We are not belligerent like the Salvadoreans', I was told.

(For decades there was hostility between El Salvador and Honduras which, in June 1969, erupted in the 'soccer war' between the two nations, El Salvador being furious at being defeated by Honduras in a World Cup eliminator. There were other reasons for the short war, but the match result seems to have been the last straw.)

Honduras, in return for considerable financial aid, has allowed itself to become the principal US military base in Central America. Large numbers of United States army and air force personnel are stationed in Honduras for training purposes and as supply headquarters for the region and also, presumably, to 'defend' Central America from communism and Marxist revolutionaries.

During my two visits we spent some time in the capital, Tegucigalpa (a busy, congested city with an airport perilously near dense and high-rise housing close to the city centre). We also managed to visit some towns, villages and parishes to the north and to the south of the country and listened, sadly, to the usual stories of poverty, oppression and fear.

Costa Rica is the most southerly of the Central American republics. Its southern border is the frontier with Panama (which, formerly part of Colombia, is not considered to be a Central American country).

Costa Rica is different from the other four Central American nations. It has no armed forces, is peaceful, relatively prosperous and with better social, educational and cultural resources than the others. Hence it does not attract human rights organisations such as CIIR.

Only once did I get to Costa Rica – for a conference about the situation elsewhere in Central America – and it seemed to live up to its reputation: orderly, clean, modern and quiet (at least compared to its neighbours).

CHAPTER TWENTY-EIGHT

Guatemala

Guatemala is a land of enchantment with a tragic history. It has natural beauty in abundance: Lake Atitlán surrounded by volcanoes is breathtakingly lovely; the Cuchumatanes mountains are like a huge wall or barrier behind which lies the mysterious district of Ixil: the historic city of Antigua was the Conquistadores' capital of all Central America; most of the people are Mayans with the women in their traditional and dazzlingly colourful costumes – what a wonderful country but what a tragic history.

My first visit to Guatemala took place in October 1984 but I have been back many times, early on as a member of CIIR delegations but, more recently, on my own to visit friends, especially Bishop Julio Cabrera Ovalle, a dedicated and fearless pastor and a dear friend.

Monseñor Cabrera was bishop of the diocese of Quiché for fifteen years (1987-2002). He had been rector of the national major seminary and then a parish priest in Guatemala City. I first met him in his diocese in 1987 (and from then on, he would introduce me as the first bishop to visit him in the 'afflicted' diocese of martyrs of which he was pastor).

Let me explain a little. Quiché is in the high plains and mountains of northwest Guatemala, with a largely indigenous population. For some years it was under martial law of the most vicious and cruel kind. The government and the army saw the people as rebellious and were determined to subdue them. This they tried to do by terror, with massacres, kidnappings, disappearances (all finally and fully catalogued in 1998 in the volumes of *Guatemala: Nunca Más*).

Specifically, the church was the principal target of the op-

pression, above all the catechists, sacristans and others active in
the parishes. The diocese of Quiché had been staffed, since its
creation in 1967, by Spanish priests, Missionaries of the Sacred
Heart. In June and July of 1980 two of them were assassinated (at
the behest of the military) and, with other assassinations threatened (including his own), the bishop of the time, Mons. Juan
Gerardi and most of the priests fled temporarily from Quiché. A
few priests remained and one of them was murdered in
February 1981.

Since the Guatemalan government refused to allow Mons.
Gerardi to re-enter Guatemala on his return from a meeting with
Pope John Paul II, the Vatican then appointed, as an interim
measure, an apostolic administrator, Mons. Pablo Urízar (whom
I met when I first went to Quiché in 1984).

To achieve a solution to the problem, Mons. Gerardi, when
permitted to return to Guatemala, did not resume as bishop of
Quiché, but was made an auxiliary bishop of Guatemala City
(where later he led the editorial team which published
Guatemala: Nunca Más and was himself assassinated in April
1998 a few days after the work was published). Bishop Gerardi
told me once that his decision to leave the diocese of Quiché
temporarily with most of the priests in 1980 was the most difficult decision of his life: he didn't know if he had done the right
thing but at least it produced worldwide publicity for the atrocities being carried out in Quiché.

With the transfer of Mons. Gerardi to Guatemala City, the
way was open for the appointment of a new bishop – and Mons.
Julio Cabrera was chosen by Rome for the post.

During my visits to Quiché, I accompanied Mons. Cabrera to
nearly all of the parishes in the vast diocese. On one occasion he
took me to the parish of Playa Grande in the area known as
Ixcán in the north of the diocese, near the Mexican border. There
is no road directly through the diocese to Playa Grande, so our
journey (in a 4 -wheel drive vehicle) took us two days and was
by road and track round, as it were, three sides of a square.
Although the military presence was still very evident, new vil-

lages and settlements were slowly springing up, many of them
peopled by those who had been refugees from the terror, some
having fled to Mexico and others, amazingly, having survived
hidden in the mountains, forests and jungles of Guatemala. The
story these internal refugees had to tell was astonishing. The
army never succeeded in capturing them. They lived in desper-
ate poverty but somehow managed to grow food, to educate
their children, to care for those who became ill. They survived
thus for years, their existence known to only a very few. Bishop
Cabrera heard about them and made a memorable visit where
he received an emotional welcome. Gradually, as conditions got
a little less dangerous, the CPRs as they were known
('*Comunidades de Población en Resistencia*') emerged from hiding
and it was some of them, as well as those who had fled to
Mexico, who were repopulating Ixcán. Conditions were very
primitive in the new settlements and I was privileged to hear
many tales of heroism amid murders, disappearances and cruelty
as well as of escapes and survival against all the odds. The
strong, simple faith of so many of these people was truly edify-
ing and their unfailing kindness was heart-warming.

I have already spoken of the area known as Ixil, to the north
of the diocese (but south of Playa Grande and Ixcán). It is hidden
behind the enormous barrier of the Cuchumatanes range and is
reached by a track that consists of hairpin bends, steep inclines
and many stretches with cliffs on one side and precipices on the
other. The views are stupendous (if you are not too frightened to
look).

Ixil has three huge parishes – Nebaj, Chajul and Cotzal, each
with many outstations. It is a beautiful area among the mountains but the people (who have their own language, different
from those further south and further north) are poor peasants
with very few educational possibilities and a history of violent
and bloody repression by the Guatemalan army. I visited Ixil
many times and became very friendly with the parish priest of
Cotzal (a German) and the parish priest of Chajul (an Italian).
All three of the parishes had had many martyrs and there had

been several instances of 'massacres', where whole communities had been murdered.

Yet, somehow or other, normal life continued despite the fear which had been added to the people's poverty-stricken daily existence. A guerilla army of sorts operated in Ixil (as in other war-torn parts of Guatemala) but without the organisation that characterised the FMLN in El Salvador or the FSLN in Nicaragua.

On one occasion, however, when the parish priest of Chajul was driving me back from Nebaj to his parish, we were stopped by a group of guerrilla fighters who suddenly emerged from the maize plants growing at the road side. They were very courteous (especially when they discovered we were priests) but explained their reasons for having taken up arms, and 'asked' (probably expecting) some help from us. On other occasions the men might have taken clothes or watches or radios or money but on that occasion they seemed satisfied with a share of the bread we had bought in Nebaj.

In Chajul the parish priest has been very active in establishing and promoting the 'Asociación Chajulense Va'l Vaq Quyol' in the parish. It is basically a co-operative of which all local small farmers and producers (whether parishioners or not) can become members. The co-operative then markets their produce, especially coffee, much more widely than the individuals could, not only in Guatemala but in the United States, Canada and Europe. Moreover, the co-operative has now gone over to organic products exclusively. This initiative has brought some prosperity to an area in which, previously, only the owners of the large estates lived above subsistence level.

After forty years of violence with, it is reckoned, 160,000 killed, the civil war in Guatemala came to an end in 1996 but unfortunately the nation has now entered another era of violence and personal danger as the result of a great wave of murders, kidnappings (particularly of children) and armed robbery. Unemployment (especially after demobilisation), drug trafficking and revenge feuds have all contributed to the wave of crime.

So Guatemala remains an uneasy country and, in my opinion, the basic reason for generations of unrest, violence and oppression is the inequality of land ownership. Relatively few families own huge amounts of the best land; millions of peasants have either a few hectares of poor land – or none at all, seeking work on the big estates in dreadful conditions and with miserable levels of pay. Moreover, through their power, their influence and widespread corruption, the rich become richer, proper land redistribution never takes place, and nothing changes.

Another powerful influence for decades has been the Latin American policy of the United States. Not only has the USA defended the interests of the estate owners (some of whom are United States multinational companies) but it has tended to condemn peasant unrest and denounce those who took up arms as agents of Communist subversion. Hence the United States has aided the Guatemalan government policy of repression by awarding huge financial grants, by sending expert military advisors and by training Guatemalan officers in counter-terrorist warfare. United States policy in Guatemala, and in Central America generally, has been interfering, shameful and immoral. The massive violation of human rights by the United States in Central America is one of the great scandals of our age, yet its perpetrators seem either unaware or, even worse, unconcerned.

On one memorable occasion in Guatemala, I spent a week in the parish of Chajul (in Ixil), visiting a number of villages in the mountains, experiencing the people's living conditions, listening to their stories, ministering to their spiritual needs. That experience I have narrated in *Guatemala: A Bishop's Journey*.

Throughout his fifteen years as bishop of the diocese of Quiché, Julio Cabrera had shown himself to be a caring, energetic, courageous and dedicated pastor. He knew the people, became aware of their culture, their problems and their sufferings, became a father to the priests and religious, fostered vocations to the priesthood, encouraged lay people to be active and involved, and was always available to everyone. Quiche was a very dangerous place but the bishop did not flinch from criticising the authorities and especially the military (his Sunday homilies were broadcast each week) and in every possible way encouraging the people in their lives of suffering and fear. On several occasions he was 'warned about his conduct' by the military and I often thought that, fearless as he was and determined to be faithful to his mission, he would be murdered.

But in fact, early in 2002, he was transferred by the Pope to the diocese of Jalapa, in south-east Guatemala, an area where there had been, over the years, a great deal less unrest and violence. He accepted the decision obediently and moved to his new diocese (accompanied by his personal staff of five remarkable indigenous ladies, two to assist in his office and three to look after the domestic arrangements). When I spent some time with him in October 2004 he had already made a great impression in Jalapa, inaugurating a new pastoral centre for the diocese and inspiring priests, religious and laity to share his pastoral zeal.

PART FIVE

Today's Church

CHAPTER TWENTY-NINE

Vatican II

The Second Vatican Council (1962-1965) was a total surprise, a cause of bewilderment and confusion, and an event whose effect has been to produce a revolution in our church, a source of deep division but also a Spirit-led pastoral renewal.

I was a member of the teaching staff at St Peter's College, Cardross (the interdiocesan seminary for Glasgow, Motherwell and Paisley dioceses) when the Council was announced and during the first three of its four sessions. (The world's bishops met for two or three months in St Peter's, Rome, each autumn from 1962 till 1965.) My early reactions, which probably many priests and others shared, were not enthusiastic. Did we need a Council? Were things not all right in the church? John XXIII seemed to have called the Council more or less on a sudden impulse while on a visit to St Paul's Basilica (on the outskirts of Rome). And was he not simply imposing on the whole church what he had already done in Venice and then, when he became Pope, in the diocese of Rome? And the decrees of those two diocesan synods, as we had heard, had been very restrictive and authoritarian.

Before the Council assembled, there had been an ante-preparatory and then a preparatory commission. Archbishop Donald Campbell of Glasgow was summoned to Rome to participate in this preparatory work. He was accompanied by two advisers, his auxiliary, Bishop James Ward, and our seminary rector, Mgr Charles Treanor. I recall that the principal documentation carried by the latter were the Sunday newspapers 'so that the students in the college in Rome would have the football reports'.

The naiveté of that Scottish delegation was by no means

unique with the result that the working papers prepared for and presented to the full Council when it met were a safe and reassuring summary of neo-Scholastic theology as taught in the Gregorian University in Rome and in many seminaries throughout the world.

At the opening of Vatican II, John XXIII spoke of 'opening windows' and '*aggiornamento*'. His address caused great interest and a certain nervousness. But more was soon to come.

Shortly after the Council got under way, a group of important European bishops (from France, Germany and the Low Countries) expressed great dissatisfaction with the working papers and the agenda set for the Council by the Preparatory Commission. Despite vehement opposition from members of the Roman Curia and some Italian bishops, the Council voted to reject the working papers and the agenda prepared for it. This was an ecclesiastical declaration of independence against the Roman Curia and its supporters, a *coup d'Eglise* that came as a complete and shocking surprise to a large number of bishops – including, one suspects, the Scottish contingent. Many bishops and indeed many Catholics (including some seminary staffs!) had been unaware of new currents of theological and pastoral thinking gaining ground in France, Germany, Holland and Belgium and that now found expression – and acceptance – in the Vatican Council.

The stage having been re-set, the Council got down to business and over the four years of activity produced some very fine pastoral decrees to guide the church's varied activities plus four 'Constitutions' which are even more important – teaching documents on the Sacred Liturgy (*Sacrosanctum Concilium*), on the Church (*Lumen Gentium*), on Divine Revelation (*Dei Verbum*) and on the Church in the Modern World (*Gaudium et Spes*). These four Constitutions were truly innovative and each in its own way has changed not only the church's teaching but the church itself. The Holy Spirit spoke through the Popes (Paul VI having succeeded John XXIII in 1963) and the bishops of the church. Have we, the church, listened?

CHAPTER THIRTY

The Ecclesiology of Vatican II

It would be foolish to attempt to put the various teaching documents of the Second Vatican Council in order of importance but surely the most basic is the Constitution *Lumen Gentium* on the Church.

Over the years since the Council I have gone through a learning curve about that Constitution and its implications as they have been developed, especially in the teaching of Pope John Paul II. The learning process has brought me joy, affirmation and a real sense of freedom.

As seminarians in Rome in the late 40s, one of our major subjects was *De Ecclesia*, taught in Latin by a Jesuit Fr Timoteo Zapalena. His Latin, spoken the Spanish way, was nearly incomprehensible to me but fortunately his lectures were all in his book.

It started by proving that the church was monarchical (the Roman Pontiff) and hierarchical (the bishops). The vision was pyramidal and legalistic – but I wouldn't blame our professor because that was the accepted theology of those days and I had no problems with it. It was the theology that sustained and justified the ministry of bishops and priests at that time and, as far as I am aware, was questioned by few, if any, 'ordinary Catholics'.

The 'schema' on the church which was prepared for and presented to the bishops at the Second Vatican Council followed these lines. To the surprise and annoyance of some bishops, especially members of the Roman Curia, it was rejected by the majority of bishops and a new draft document was demanded.

That new document was *Lumen Gentium*. It still speaks of the hierarchical nature of the church and the teaching authority of

124

pope and bishops – but that is in chapter 3. The start of the Constitution is on 'the mystery of the church' (viz. it is God's kingdom on earth, inaugurated but not yet fully achieved, poor, persecuted, imperfect yet possessing the Holy Spirit) and the second chapter treats of 'the People of God' (i.e. all of us who are baptised members of the church). There are later chapters on the laity (dealt with positively and not contrasted with clergy in a negative way) and on the universal call to holiness in the church.

The Council's teaching on the church was new for most of us in Scotland. It was refreshing and, at the same time, seemed daring, indeed revolutionary. Yet it is the teaching of an ecumenical council of pope and the world's bishops and so is certain and reliable. Since 1964 (when *Lumen Gentium* was published) much authoritative teaching has been based on it, especially many documents from John Paul II (*Christifideles Laici* of 1988, his letters announcing and concluding the Millennium Jubilee Year, and his letter for the start of the third Christian millennium.)

How much influence has all this had on our thinking and on our behaviour as members of the church? A considerable amount, I think, but not yet enough. For example, what do we mean when we ask 'What is the church doing about it?'; again do we still assume that, somehow, priests and nuns should be (and are) holier than 'ordinary' people? Do we still see priests (and I suppose bishops) as if they were on pedestals? Is baptism properly recognised as the moment of God's greatest gift to us?

It cannot be denied that increasingly in recent post-conciliar years the Holy See itself has attracted criticism on such grounds as excessive centralisation, unwillingness to allow decisions to be made locally, an apparent lack of trust in regard to bishops and bishops' conferences, a Roman Curia which seems to take more and more power to itself and so on. Furthermore, such criticisms are being voiced by responsible people, experienced bishops some of them, and should not be ignored. Let me develop this.

I describe, when writing about ICEL (International Commission on English in the Liturgy), the unseemly way in which, in recent years, the Congregation for Divine Worship and Discipline of the Sacraments has treated not only the agency of English-speaking Bishops' Conferences (ICEL) but directly the conferences themselves.

The appointment of bishops is another area of discontent, both in the manner in which this is carried out (secretly and by Rome itself without any genuine discussion with the local church or the local conference of bishops) and in some appointments that have been made, especially in North and Latin America, as well as for some of the larger dioceses elsewhere. Rome's regulation that it alone will choose who are to be bishops is not traditional or historic. Moreover, there appears to be an agenda that often favours appointments of men who are conservative and not in tune with Vatican II and its ecclesiology.

There has also been quite an amount of disappointment over the way in which Synods of Bishops have developed. These Synods were begun in order to continue the ethos of collegiality generated by the Second Vatican Council. The idea was that a certain number of bishops, representing their conferences from all over the world, should be convened in Rome every two or three years in order to deliberate on one or more topics of importance to the church e.g. Penance and Reconciliation, Priesthood, Consecrated Life, Laity.

However, after a few Synods it became clear that they were only consultative and not deliberative – they would not be allowed to make decisions or offer teaching. Further and even within these narrow parameters, it seemed that the Roman Curia was manipulating the process in the sense that, at certain stages of the Synod process when choices had to be made, those choices were made not by the Synod bishops nor by the conferences but by the Synod officials and in secret. They were thus able to 'censor' those topics which were 'inconvenient'.

For example, bishops' conferences are asked to make suggestions for the Synod's '*Instrumentum Laboris*' (working document) but the document is compiled by the Roman officials; it is they also who decide the agenda for the small groups into which the

Synod divides for its second part; it is they who, from the reports of the small groups, decide the final report presented to the Holy Father; and it is he, not the Synod, who writes the 'Apostolic Exhortation' (which is the only document which is made public from the Synod). The effectiveness of the Synod is further limited because, during the plenary sessions which take up the first part, each bishop can make only one short speech – but these speeches are not in any logical order and there is no public discussion allowed of any proposals or suggestions made in the speeches.

Many bishops now feel that the Synods are so controlled that their effectiveness has been severely diminished and they serve little purpose.

Perhaps it is a less important matter, but I have always felt that the daily newspaper of the Holy See, 'L'Osservatore Romano', is more of an official bulletin than a true newspaper. The news that it contains is always favourable to the church and so are the articles. Real controversy, criticism of the church and adult discussion of its problems are absent from its columns and the impression is given of manipulated content by a fortress mentality out of touch with the real world.

There is, nevertheless, one very important aspect of this whole matter to be kept in mind – the need to preserve unity of teaching in the church. Certainly present practice of centralisation is an *effective* way of achieving this, but is it the *right* way? The difficulties which the worldwide Anglican Communion is experiencing in trying to have unity in such matters as the appointment of practising homosexuals and the ordination of women shows the danger of a lack of a firm central authority. If Rome relaxed its stance and devolved more authority and decisions to local churches would that inevitably lead to disunity in teaching?

That is a question perhaps impossible to answer with any assurance. One hopes that the Holy Spirit guides not only the bishop of Rome but all bishops and indeed all the baptised. And this touches on a disputed ecclesiological question: which has priority, the worldwide Catholic Church from which the local churches derive their validity, or the local churches which are in communion with each other and with the bishop of Rome to form the worldwide church?

The extent of decentralisation, using the principle of subsidiarity, that would be best is a matter for discussion. But that there should be more than at present, I think is right and necessary and widely hoped for.

Vatican II teaching on ecclesiology challenges us and we should be aware of it and embrace it not only in theory but in practice too. That applies to everyone in the church. Please God we may increasingly understand and try to implement the Council's inspired ecclesiology.

CHAPTER THIRTY-ONE

The Local Church after Vatican II

The most disturbing document of the Second Vatican Council is the Constitution *Lumen Gentium* on the church. Disturbing in the sense that it was meant to change us, to change the church. Has it? Is the local church changed? Are we, individual Catholics, changed?

Well, it depends. In theory, the church is changed. Some local churches are changed (or slowly changing) and it is the same with individual members. Some are changed, some not; some think they have changed; some think they have not changed ...

Even though the essentials of Mass remain unchanged, the way in which we celebrate Mass is very different from what it was in pre-Vatican II days. That is so evident as to make further explanation unnecessary and tedious. But that everyone in the church is called to be holy, to be active (using the gifts received through baptism and confirmation), to seek to make the local church a true community, indeed a communion of sharers in the one and only priesthood of Christ – is this Vatican II teaching a reality in parishes yet? The Council also radically advanced the Catholic Church's views on ecumenism, on our relations with non-Christians, on the role we should have in today's world. Have these ideas been accepted and put into practice yet?

Through the sacraments of Christian initiation we are full members of the church, gifted, empowered, with rights and re-sponsibilities. Yet there are many Catholics who are unaware of this and therefore not actively involved. There are many, also, who show such deference to priests that the relationship, if not one of fear, can be something approaching infantilism and ser-vility. Of course I am not recommending an absence of law and order etc, for collaborative ministry does not mean chaos.

Besides, infantile servility or fear in lay people doesn't help a priest. Most priests feel frustrated in such circumstances and a few of us may, God forgive us, relapse into clericalism ('only the priest has the right to decide'), paternalism ('I know better than you do') or, worse still, hypocrisy or pomposity. Yes, we can be tempted if we are spoiled by misplaced respect.

Most Catholics nowadays worry about falling numbers – fewer people at Mass, fewer vocations to priesthood and religious life, fewer marriages, fewer children (and incidentally, less income for parishes and dioceses at a time of increasing expenses). These concerns produce explanations galore and (fewer) solutions – materialism, individualism, relativism, selfishness, hedonism, influence of the media, peer pressure, we should pray more, have less boring Masses, do more for youth and for families, provide better marriage preparation.

I do not want to discuss these explanations or remedies. There are other occasions to do so, occasions, I am afraid, to make ourselves feel depressed or guilty. Let us be content with saying that we are aware of these negative developments, that we regret them and are not complacent but that we shall simply try to give witness to what we believe, to the faith we have received – and leave the situation in the hands of the God who is in charge and in whom we trust.

'Jesus said, "Do you also want to go away?" Simon Peter answered, "Lord, to whom shall we go? You have the message of eternal life and we believe".'

CHAPTER THIRTY-TWO

ICEL

An important task that came my way as bishop was to be the Scottish representative on the Episcopal Board of ICEL. The International Commission on English in the Liturgy was established by English-speaking Bishops' Conferences during the Second Vatican Council when it became obvious that the vernacular languages would be permitted in the liturgy. Since the recommendation was that there should be one translation for countries using the same language, an organisation like ICEL was needed, a mixed commission with representatives from the various Bishops' Conferences requiring English translations.

The basic work in ICEL was done by teams of experts in various disciplines, charged with the responsibility of producing translations that would be faithful to the Latin original – but not so literal as to be stilted; and suitable for proclamation and for public prayer. The translators' work was examined and, if necessary, revised by an Advisory Committee which then passed their texts to the Episcopal Board (eleven bishops each representing his Bishops' Conference: Australia, Canada, England and Wales, India, Ireland, New Zealand, Pakistan, Philippines, Scotland, Southern Africa and the United States of America). Once the Episcopal Board had approved the texts, they were sent to the Bishops' Conferences. Each Conference could then give formal approval (with any changes if it felt they were required; formal rejection was also possible). Finally the Conference, when satisfied, would send the document to the Roman Congregation for Divine Worship and Discipline of the Sacraments seeking *recognitio*; once this last was given, the text could be published for use in that particular country.

That summarises the process but it was a process that demanded and received meticulous attention by many experts and authorities, debate and discussion and possible admission of amendments or alternative translations – a long, careful and demanding process.

The documents which ICEL translated comprised the rites of all the sacraments, the various liturgical books (RCIA, reconciliation, care of the sick, funerals …) but, of course, the principal texts were those of the Roman Missal (the unchanging 'Order of Mass', prefaces, eucharistic prayers, presidential prayers for Sundays, feasts, commons, votive Masses) – an enormous production of more than 2,000 texts even without the scripture readings (which ICEL did not translate as various versions in English already exist and from which each Conference makes its choice).

During the years that I was involved with ICEL, most of our work was on the revised translation of the Missal. The first English translation, issued in 1973, needed revision because it had been done very quickly. The language was spare, the style sometimes 'bitty', and it was clear that, in many parts of it, more accurate translations could be made. In addition to its translating work, ICEL had also been charged with providing 'original texts' i.e. not translations of Latin texts, but directly composed in English, especially for the Alternative Opening Prayers on Sundays and for new votive Masses.

As an Episcopal Board member and, later, as one of the three-man Executive Committee of the Board, I was frequently throughout each year sent bundles of texts for study and report. So our work was by no means limited to our annual meetings in Washington.

ICEL had its headquarters in that city where the ICEL Secretariat (six or seven persons headed by the Executive Secretary) did wonderful things not only in managing the work of all the experts and bishops but also in providing us with background information and advice, the result of their intimate knowledge of the history of the Latin liturgy, of the situation regarding other languages (French, German, Italian, Spanish, Portuguese) and of the particular problems and possibilities associated with the various texts. I found the work extremely interesting, even fascinating; very time-consuming but time given gladly because we were serving English-speaking Catholics all over the world.

There was another aspect that made me very happy – the comradeship that grew up among us, bishops, priests, religious, lay people, men and women. We came from a variety of countries, we had a wide range of skills and expertise and we respected each other's work and enjoyed each other's company, especially when we met. I miss the work and the meetings but, thanks be to God, the friendships and the occasional contacts continue.

By the time our work on the revised translation of the Missal was completed in 1997, I had succeeded Archbishop Daniel Pilarczyk of Cincinnati as chairman of the Episcopal Board of ICEL. The various English-speaking Bishops' Conferences were sent the finished product and all but one approved it with overwhelming majorities; the one exception was the United States. A minority of the bishops of that Conference did vote against the revised translation but, even so, the majority there was sufficiently large to secure its approval for the whole nation.

However, the entire scene was to change and our revised translation, on which we had worked so hard and of which we were proud, was to be rejected, not by the Bishops' Conferences but by Rome.

The problem became apparent in 1996 with the arrival of the Chilean Cardinal Jorge Arturo Medina Estévez to be Prefect (i.e. head) of the Roman Congregation for Divine Worship and Discipline of the Sacraments. Although with some previous prefects relations between the Congregation and ICEL had been strained, the difficulties were to do with specific matters. For some years before Cardinal Medina, relations were cordial and ICEL had some useful and very friendly meetings in Rome with officials of the Congregation.

Whether due to Cardinal Medina or whether only concomitant with his appointment, things changed and at ICEL we began to feel very threatened. The change, as I say, may have been of the Cardinal's making or he may have been advised, either by higher authority or by some Congregation officials, to 'bring ICEL to heel'.

At any rate, I (as ICEL chairman) began to receive letters from Cardinal Medina, couched in formal, seemingly courteous language, either deploring some of ICEL's activities or 'requesting' changes or announcing new regulations. Letters were exchanged between us, the tone was always superficially polite in an old-fashioned way but there was no real dialogue or attempt to hear our views and consider them. Decisions had been made, consultation was not on the agenda.

I remember one occasion in particular when I wrote to the Cardinal to say that I would be happy to go to Rome if he would be willing to meet me. The reply was that, as a bishop I was welcome to go to Rome and he would receive me – as he would any bishop – but I would not be received as chairman of ICEL to discuss its concerns.

(Some years earlier I did have a private meeting with the Cardinal but discussion was difficult as he does not speak English and conversation in Spanish about translation from Latin to English is not very satisfactory. So perhaps the snub to which I have referred merely avoided another frustrating encounter.)

What is good translation? A simple question but not an easy one to answer. Fidelity and accuracy to what is being translated, yes; but also the result must be acceptable for those who have to use it. The two extremes, both unacceptable, are, first, a translation that is so 'word for word' that it is stilted and artificial; and, second, a translation that is so 'free' that it is paraphrase rather than translation. The good translation, and this is true for the liturgy as well as everything else, lies somewhere between the two extremes.

To enable the translators to know just where the right 'middle way' lies, some authoritative guidance is necessary. This guidance was provided until 2001 by a document issued in 1969 by the 'Consilium' established by the Holy See after Vatican II for this – and other – reasons. The document is called *Instruction on Translation of Liturgical Texts* and was used by ICEL in its work.

Although there were rumours that another document was under preparation in Rome, ICEL was told by Congregation officials that work done before its publication, including the revised translation of the Missal, would be judged not by its norms but by those of the 1969 Instruction.

After a long delay, the new document, called *Liturgiam Authenticam* (from the first two words of its Latin text), was finally published in May 2001 – after ICEL's revised Missal had been completed and approved by the English-speaking Bishops' Conferences. Despite previous assurances, ICEL was told that the revised Missal was subject to its norms! This seemed not only like changing the goalposts but changing them after the game was over. Or again, if a new 30 mph speed limit is introduced on a road, should motorists who, before the new law is enacted or known, exceeded that limit, be found guilty of its infringement?

Liturgiam Authenticam is a long and prolix document, produced without any consultation either with mixed commissions such as ICEL, or even with Bishops' Conferences. It is a document that has been widely and severely criticised. It certainly requires translation from Latin to be closer to 'word for word' rather than a somewhat freer style that is faithful to the meaning and sense of the Latin but nearer an English that is both intelligible and usable, prayerful and proclaimable.

In addition to its stricter norms for translation, *Liturgiam Authenticam* also lays down rules for mixed commissions such as ICEL; for example, all those who work for ICEL must, unless they are bishops, have prior authorisation from the Roman Congregation; only translation work may be undertaken and not, as hitherto, the composition of original extra prayers even if requested by Bishops' Conferences; ecumenical contacts have to be discontinued.

These developments took place against a background of expressions of dismay from many liturgical and theological scholars and, on the other side, of attacks on ICEL (especially from a number of very conservative publications and letters) which condemned the mixed commission as anything from arrogant and disobedient to heretical.

I realise that, as a leading member of ICEL, I tend to see the dispute from one point of view. Was the Congregation justified in its denial of its *recognitio* to the revised translation of the Missal and in its generally hostile and very critical attitude to ICEL? Opinions do, and will, vary on this. In order to be as fair as I think possible, let me say that ICEL may sometimes have appeared intolerant or arrogant (but ICEL did use the very best people it could find – liturgists, theologians, scripture scholars, Latinists, English writers – and in this sense its scholarly resources were second to none and inevitably superior to those which the Congregation for Divine Worship could employ). Again, one could admit that, apart from their one bishop representative on ICEL's Episcopal Board, some Bishops' Conferences did not normally take an active part in ICEL's work; but neither did the Congregation, despite our frequent invitations to do so. In fact, various 'Progress Reports' were issued by ICEL – we were not secretive about our work – and these reports were sent to Bishops' Conferences and also to Rome. If our work was so unacceptable to Rome, why was it not stopped sooner? Or why, at least, were we not contacted?

Wherever the blame lies, the whole business has been extremely sad and, to those who are aware of its details, unedifying and even scandalous. Many years' serious work has been wasted and still the people wait, bewildered by the delay, for the promised revised Missal in English.

Radical changes took place in ICEL's statutes, leadership and procedures at the Episcopal Board meeting in July 2002. Both the Chairman (myself) and the Executive Secretary (Dr John Page) left ICEL, the latter resigning because he felt he could not continue under the new ways of working and I not standing for re-elec-

tion because I was 76 years old and due to retire as bishop of the
diocese; I felt that it was not appropriate for ICEL to be led by a
retired bishop, especially one with cancer. Unfortunately, it so
happened that, at the same meeting, several of the Episcopal
Board were newcomers. Nevertheless, the Board elected a new
chairman, a new executive secretary and a new executive committee of the Episcopal Board, abolished the Consultants' (formerly Advisory) Committee (as required by the Congregation)
and accepted all the directives in *Liturgiam Authenticam.* We
shall have to wait for a revised Missal but look forward to it
eagerly and with our good wishes to those who have the task of
producing it.

I have already spoken about the activities of the Roman
Congregation for Divine Worship and about its criticisms of
ICEL. I have also said that there are those who consider those
criticisms to be justified.

However, there is another player in the drama – the English-
speaking Bishops' Conferences. I believe that they ought to have
played a much stronger part in the whole affair and not only because they had all approved the ICEL revised translation of the
Missal yet, without any complaint or question, allowed the
Congregation, in denying its *recognitio*, to overturn their approval. The *recognitio* is not the same as a further 'approval'; it is
rather 'ratification' and is supposed to be only a way in which
the Congregation recognises the Conferences' decision and ac-
cepts it (or not – but this last merely and only for very serious
reasons such as heresy or similar grave error). Moreover,
Liturgiam Authenticam arrogates to the Congregation certain
powers which properly belong to the Conferences, especially
the right to set up mixed commissions such as ICEL, to approve
their statutes, their personnel, their programmes and their way
of working. All of these duties are declared by *Liturgiam
Authenticam* to belong to the Congregation – and the Bishops'
Conferences have meekly accepted this.

Not only is all this against the original statutes of ICEL but it
goes against the ecclesiology that was taught by Vatican II:

collegiality, the authority of bishops (who are not merely Rome's branch managers), subsidiarity. Much has been written in recent years of the increasing power which the Roman Curia is giving itself – and all this is a further example of the centralisation of authority (or, if you like, power).

In my opinion, things need to be rectified to recapture the spirit and the teaching of the Second Vatican Council. Ecclesiology is the main problem (and the liturgical situation is a sad illustration of the problem). And specifically, the Roman Curia needs that reform which recent Popes have acknowledged but not achieved.

EPILOGUE

Retirement

A retired bishop used to be an unusual thing. Bishops just kept on as diocesan leaders until death. But since the introduction of the new *Code of Canon Law* in 1983, 'a diocesan bishop who has completed his seventy-fifth year of age is requested to offer his resignation from office to the Supreme Pontiff who, taking all the circumstances into account, will make provision accordingly' (Canon 401#1).

I offered my resignation to the Holy Father in a letter dated 6 May 2001 (having reached seventy-five on the previous day). My resignation was soon accepted with the phrase *nunc pro tunc*, i.e. accepted but to be effective later. In fact, I ceased to be bishop of Galloway only when my successor's appointment was published on 7 April 2004.

The following month, in *The Galloway Newsletter* for May 2004, I gave my retiring reflections:

Going, Going, (Almost) Gone!
Since the announcement, on 7 April, that Pope John Paul II had appointed Mgr John Cunningham as my successor, many people have congratulated me on my retirement (after a delay lasting almost three years, since I became seventy-five on 5 May 2001).Usually, people added, 'You must be delighted' but a few have asked whether I am sad to be retiring. That question challenges me.

I want to say that I truly welcome my retirement, partly for my sake and certainly for the sake of the diocese. Not only will the diocese benefit from new and fresh leadership but the uncertainty that has lasted three years has been unsettling (especially for the priests) and the appointment of a new bishop is long overdue.

For these reasons (and because Mgr Cunningham is such an excellent choice), I am very happy that my retirement has come at last.

It would be wrong, however, not to admit to some feelings of sadness that my years as bishop of this wonderful diocese are over. But instead of sadness I prefer to thank God for all the happiness and fulfilment I have had and for the prospect of having so many memories to enjoy in the days ahead.

Memories of ordaining priests, which I always found an awesome privilege. Memories of the annual Mass of Chrism when the cathedral church of the Good Shepherd is filled to overflowing and the liturgy is celebrated with such deep emotion (especially when the priests solemnly and publicly renew their commitment to serve the people). Memories of the Whithorn pilgrimage in sunshine and rain, in calm and storm, always a physical effort but richly symbolic as we of today recognise the antiquity and tradition of the diocese to which we belong.

Visits to parishes brought me great pleasure, whether for confirmation (and also, latterly, first communion) or jubilees and anniversaries or simply pastoral visits which I tried to carry out each weekend since 1981. Annual visits to schools were happy occasions ('Who's your teacher?' 'Fine!') but quite demanding. Diocesan pilgrimages to the Holy Land and to Lourdes were unfailingly rewarding, not only because we were in holy places but also because of the bonds of friendship and support that so rapidly developed.

I have been fortunate enough to get to know several countries in Latin America and to experience their poverty, their faith and their friendship. Nor must I forget the privilege of my association with the International Commission on English in the Liturgy (ICEL) which involved a great deal of fascinating work, becoming friends with many fine people from all over the English-speaking world and, ultimately, the disappointment of having our work approved by all the Bishops' Conferences which ICEL serves but then rejected by the Congregation for Divine Worship in Rome.

Perhaps most of all my memory will be of people – you, the priests, religious and lay people, young and old, of this diocese who have been so supportive, so co-operative, so forgiving, so good to me. I am truly happy to have been your bishop and I am happy that, for the time that remains to me, I shall continue to live in this diocese whose people I have grown to love so much.

Retired bishops in the past were 'transferred' to 'titular sees *in partibus infidelium*', i.e. dioceses that no longer existed. Now that somewhat coy fiction has been abandoned and 'a bishop whose resignation from office has been accepted acquires the title "emeritus" of his diocese.' (Canon 402 #1)

The word sounds fitting and worthy, perhaps something like 'meritorious'. So I looked up my Latin dictionary: '*emeritus* – one who has served his time, a veteran, unfit for service, worn out.'

So that's what I am! It just goes to confirm the old adage that no one is indispensable. Ah, well! So be it. Amen.